Contents

WHO/CHD/98.9
DISTR.: GENERAL
ORIGINAL: ENGLISH

Evidence for the
Ten Steps to Successful Breastfeeding

DIVISION OF CHILD HEALTH AND DEVELOPMENT

World Health Organization
Geneva
1998

© World Health Organization 1998

Cover illustration adapted from a poster by permission of the Ministry of Health, Peru.

Acknowledgements

The authors of this review were Dr Constanza Vallenas and Dr Felicity Savage. Valuable assistance for the analysis was provided by Dr Jose Martines.

Many thanks are due to the following people for reviewing the document in draft and for providing helpful, constructive criticism: Ms Helen Armstrong (UNICEF, New York), Ms Beverley Chalmers (Ontario), Dr Gülbin Gokçay (University of Istanbul), Dr Rukshana Haider (International Centre for Diarrhoeal Disease Research, Bangladesh), Ms Elizabeth Kylberg (Uppsala University), Ms Ludmila Lhotská (UNICEF, New York), Dr Nancy G. Powers (University of Kansas), Professor Mary Renfrew (University of Leeds), Dr Wendelin Slusser (University of California, Los Angeles), Dr Cesar G. Victora (Federal University of Pelotas), Dr Michael Woolridge (University of Leeds).

Thanks also to members of WHO's Technical Working Group on Breastfeeding representing other units: Mrs R Saadeh, Nutrition Programme, and Dr J Zupan, Division of Reproductive Health (Technical Support) who made helpful comments. Thanks are also due to Dr Chessa Lutter (Food and Nutrition Program, PAHO/WHO) for her valuable comments, and Dr Nadia Meyer for reviewing the list of references.

EVIDENCE FOR THE
TEN STEPS TO SUCCESSFUL BREASTFEEDING

INTRODUCTION

The "Ten Steps to Successful Breastfeeding" are the foundation of the WHO/UNICEF Baby Friendly Hospital Initiative (BFHI). They summarize the maternity practices necessary to support breastfeeding. The purpose of this document is to review the evidence for the efficacy of the 'Ten Steps', and to provide a tool for both advocacy and education. It is hoped that policies and practices in future will be based on research rather than on conjecture and custom (Inch & Garforth, 1989).

There are a number of papers which present the rationale for some or all of the 'Ten Steps' (Perez-Escamilla et al, 1994; Saadeh & Akré, 1996) but there remains a need for a comprehensive and critical review of available evidence.

The BFHI was developed to promote implementation of the second operational target of the Innocenti Declaration:

> Ensure that every facility providing maternity services fully practises all ten of the **Ten Steps to Successful Breastfeeding** set out in the joint WHO/UNICEF statement 'Protecting, promoting and supporting breast-feeding: the special role of maternity services',

and aspects relevant to health facilities of the third operational target:

> Take action to give effect to the principles and aim of all Articles of the International Code of Marketing of Breast-milk Substitutes and subsequent relevant World Health Assembly [WHA] resolutions in their entirety.

The Innocenti Declaration was adopted by the Forty-fifth World Health Assembly in May 1992 in Resolution WHA 45.34.

The BFHI addresses a major factor which has contributed to the erosion of breastfeeding - that is, health care practices which interfere with breastfeeding. Until practices improve, attempts to promote breastfeeding outside the health service will be impeded. Although inappropriate maternity care cannot be held solely responsible for low exclusive breastfeeding rates, appropriate care may be a prerequisite for raising them.

Many other factors affect how women feed their infants and the length of time for which they breasfeed. These have been extensively reviewed by Popkin et al (1983), Forman (1984), Simopoulos & Grave (1984), Koktürk & Zetterström (1989), Wilmoth & Elder (1995), and include: 1) living environment (urban or rural), 2) socioeconomic status, 3) maternal education (Forman, 1984), 4) the woman's employment situation, and 5) commercial pressures, and knowledge and availability of breastmilk substitutes (Huffman, 1984). Sociocultural factors also determine beliefs and attitudes, as well as practices, related to breastfeeding. A woman's decision about infant feeding may be influenced by the perceived or actual attitudes of the child's father (Freed, Fraley & Schanler, 1993), other family members, and friends; and the amount of support she may have to carry her decision through.

The factors which affect breastfeeding rates are not only many and complex, but they operate differently in different situations. For example, the influence of a child's father may depend on the extent to which in that society a woman's male partner has control over her body; maternal education has been associated with higher breastfeeding rates in industrialized countries and with lower rates in developing countries (Forman, 1984).

Factors may also vary with time in the same community, and partial and exclusive breastfeeding may have different determinants (Perez-Escamilla et al, 1993). Cultural attitudes towards breasts as sexual symbols, and women's confidence in their ability to lactate may also differ and influence mothers' attitudes toward breastfeeding. It would not be surprising therefore to learn that implementation of the 'Ten Steps' affects breastfeeding differently in different communities. The studies reviewed here do show some differences, but these are mainly of degree rather than of direction. There are more publications from industrialized than from developing countries, but the available evidence indicates that implementation of the 'Ten Steps' in maternity facilities can increase breastfeeding in almost any setting. Implementing each Step by itself has some effect, but implementing all of them together can be expected to have a greater effect, while omitting one or more may limit the impact of those that are in place.

Thus, although to achieve adequate and sustained increases in breastfeeding, many other programme components are needed - including employment legislation, widespread public education, community support, and implementation of the International Code of Marketing of Breast-milk Substitutes (the Code) - improved health care practices are fundamental. As summarized in the 'Ten Steps', policy development and staff training resulting in appropriate skilled support of mothers before, during and after delivery, and ongoing postnatal support in the community, are all necessary to realize the improvements aimed for by other activities.

Methods used in the review

A literature search was conducted to identify published studies relating to each of the 'Ten Steps', and the effect on breastfeeding of their implementation inside health facilities. Exceptionally studies assessing interventions outside health facilities were included. Although the main purpose of the BFHI is to increase breastfeeding rates, other outcomes are also important, both in their own right, and because they may influence decisions about giving supplementary feeds. Therefore publications relating to outcomes such as infant weight change, bilirubin levels, and sleep patterns, were also identified.

As far as possible, only randomized controlled ('experimental') studies, and controlled studies where allocation was systematic or when a 'before and after intervention' design was used ('quasi-experimental') have been included. They were assessed according to certain pre-established criteria (Blum & Feachem, 1983; Perez-Escamilla et al, 1994).

2

Limitations identified for each experimental or quasi-experimental study are listed in the tables of comparative results, in the first column, and are numbered according to the following list.

Major limitations of internal validity:
1. Inadequate control: no baseline data or between-group differences not considered during analysis.
2. Confounding variables not controlled: such as maternal age, maternal education, socioeconomic status.
3. Self-selection of participants: breastfeeding outcomes may differ depending on mother's motivation to accept or reject an intervention.
4. More than 10% attrition rate (proportion lost to follow-up), unevenly distributed between intervention and control groups.
5. Undetermined internal validity: unreported attrition, poorly documented methodology or unpublished brief communication.

Minor limitations of experimental or quasi-experimental studies:
6. One-to-one comparison: when assessing a group-based intervention such as education, any difference found by comparing results of one group (ward, nursery) with another group may not reflect actual effects of the intervention. The strength of evidence is reduced.
7. Long recall period: few data about recall periods relating specifically to breastfeeding exist. Margen et al (1991) reported from a study in Mexico that "...the overall recall bias [at 3 months of feeding practices at 2 weeks] was towards mothers remembering more breastfeeding and less bottle-feeding than they had actually practiced earlier". A time lapse greater than 6 months was considered unsatisfactory for the purposes of this review.
8. Unclear definition of breastfeeding indicators:
   - 'exclusive' or 'sole' breastfeeding was considered as 'full breastfeeding' if not defined, or if defined differently from WHO indicators.
   - 'breastfeeding' was considered as 'any breastfeeding' if not defined.
9. Based on planned breastfeeding behaviour as opposed to actual practice. This reduces the strength of evidence but does not invalidate it.

Most studies do not provide information about long-term effects of health interventions. This may mask negative effects of inadequate practices, since it is currently observed that once infants start bottle-feeding the practice is only exceptionally reversed. So a difference in outcomes between 2 groups may become apparent only after several months. For that reason, the measurement of long-term breastfeeding outcomes was considered a favourable feature of a study.

A small sample size may be a limitation when a study compares 'treatments' (interventions) to try to identify the one that provides the best results. A large number of strictly selected individuals increases the probability of the results being generally ('externally') applicable. When a study intends to look for the cause and effect relationship between a practice and an outcome the experimental conditions (inclusion and exclusion criteria, baseline and follow-up variables) must be as rigorous as possible. The sample size should be large enough to detect statistically significant results between treatment and control groups and should be based on biologically meaningful differences.

3

In the field of infant feeding it is particularly difficult to randomize treatment groups. Therefore, in this review, it was considered necessary to include also non-randomized prospective cohort studies.

Criteria for including prospective cohort studies were: large sample size, control of selection bias, low proportion lost to follow-up, lost individuals similar to the rest, adequate data collection and, if possible, use of multivariate or regression analysis to control for possible confounders. Cross-sectional or retrospective studies were included if they provided useful observational information and were not seriously methodologically flawed. The measurement of long-term effects on breastfeeding duration was also considered favourable.

Presentation of information

The information is presented for each step in the following order:
1. The Global Criteria for the step, as defined for the WHO/UNICEF Baby Friendly Hospital Initiative (1992).
2. An introduction describing the background situation.
3. Evidence from experimental or quasi-experimental studies for breastfeeding outcomes, in historical order. Studies with fewer limitations are discussed in greater detail. Limitations of studies are presented separately in the comparative tables.
4. Additional supportive evidence from prospective (longitudinal) or cross-sectional studies.
5. Experimental or supportive evidence for other outcomes.
6. Discussion and conclusions.
7. A comparative table of experimental or quasi-experimental studies, when available, and/or of longitudinal or cross-sectional studies providing supportive evidence. Year of publication, country or area where study was conducted, population characteristics and methodological limitations of the study are included to provide a perspective of comparison among studies. Methodological limitations are numbered according to the list presented in the above section. Results presented include the indicator considered (exclusive, full or any breastfeeding) in relation to duration.
8. The information of one study per step is presented graphically.

The final section presents reports of combined interventions. Studies with several major limitations were excluded.

The Ten Steps to Successful Breastfeeding

Every facility providing maternity services and care for
newborn infants should:

1. Have a written breastfeeding policy that is routinely
    communicated to all health care staff.

2. Train all health care staff in skills necessary to
    implement this policy.

3. Inform all pregnant women about the benefits and
    management of breastfeeding.

4. Help mothers initiate breastfeeding within a half-hour
    of birth.

5. Show mothers how to breastfeed, and how to maintain
    lactation even if they should be separated from their
    infants.

6. Give newborn infants no food or drink other than
    breastmilk, unless *medically* indicated.

7. Practice rooming-in -- allow mothers and infants to
    remain together -- 24 hours a day.

8. Encourage breastfeeding on demand.

9. Give no artificial teats or pacifiers (also called dummies
    or soothers) to breastfeeding infants.

10. Foster the establishment of breastfeeding support
    groups and refer mothers to them on discharge from
    the hospital or clinic.

STEP 1

1.1 **"Have a written breastfeeding policy that is routinely communicated to all health care staff."**

The health facility should have a written breastfeeding policy that addresses all 10 steps and protects breastfeeding...[it] should be available so that all staff who take care of mothers and babies can refer to it... should be visibly posted in all areas of the health care facility which serve mothers, infants, and/or children...and should be displayed in the language(s) most commonly understood by patients and staff. (The Global Criteria for the WHO/UNICEF Baby Friendly Hospital Initiative, 1992)

1.2 **Introduction**

A consistent and sustained improvement in hospital practices is most likely to be achieved if there are appropriate and specific institutional policies, preferably as a standing requirement of the routine audit cycle within the facility. Policies may be written, or they may exist and be implicit without being written. Unwritten policies can be strong and effective, and written policies may be ignored. However, to effect change in the face of divergent opinion, and to sustain it when staff changes, a policy needs to be written.

Thus this step requires:
1) Appropriate policies on all practices concerning breastfeeding agreed between relevant authorities
2) Those policies to be made explicit in a written document
3) All staff and patients to be made aware of the policies.

In addition, authorities both inside a health facility (such as administrators and senior clinical staff) and outside (for example in the Ministry of Health) must be committed to the policies and must enforce them. Lack of such committment and cooperation from senior staff can be a major obstacle to consistent implementation of the 'Ten Steps'. Ideally policies should also come as a commitment from parents, health professionals, the mass media, and other community groups. Lack of commitment appears to be stronger in certain private hospitals where practices are guided by clients' comfort and financial considerations rather than long-term health benefits.

1.3 **Effectiveness of breastfeeding policies**

It is difficult to use an experimental design to show that policies effect change (Janovsky & Cassels, 1996). Descriptive and qualitative studies of experiences in different health services are more useful ways to show relationships between strong or weak policies and good or poor practices, and may be the best source of information to guide policy development.

More common than an absence of policy is a mixture of some that are appropriate and some that are inappropriate in the same service, and weakness or inconsistency in their implementation. There may be confusion about interpretation, and there may be

6

incompatibilities, such that different practices interfere with each other.

Westphal et al (1995) assessed the effectiveness of training a core team on changes in hospital breastfeeding practices in Brazil. Hospitals where trained teams worked improved their practices. However, it was acknowledged that a lack of coordination existed between policy-makers, administrators and health care staff in every facility.

To improve the effectiveness of a breastfeeding policy appropriate practices must be included, all staff must comply with it, and relevant outcomes should be monitored or audited in order to get feedback for further policy development.

1.4   Results of weak policies

Reiff & Essock-Vitale (1985) reported a survey in a university hospital in the United States of America (USA) where most official policies, educational materials and counselling and support programmes promoted breastfeeding. However, there was no policy to limit the use of infant formula, and a single brand of ready-to-use infant formula was used daily in the maternity ward. In the delivery room 66% of mothers had stated a preference for exclusive breastfeeding but when interviewed at 2 weeks only 23% were breastfeeding without formula supplements. 93% of the mothers using formula at 2 weeks knew the name of the hospital brand and 88% were using it. Thus, lack of a policy on one step may interfere with the effect of implementing the others.

Winikoff et al (1986) observed institutional constraints on breastfeeding in a hospital in the USA. Breastfeeding mothers and infants were often separated for long periods and the infants were given formula despite written policies to the contrary. There was confusion about which drugs, when given to the mother, might be contraindicated with breastfeeding and about the identification of breastfeeding mothers. A programme which included staff training, development of educational materials, and institution of a breastfeeding counselling service had a limited effect, possibly because no specific effort was made to change policies. The authors concluded that two elements were essential to achieve change: professional education, and the willingness of administrative staff to re-evaluate policies and the practices to which they refer.

Garforth & Garcia (1989) surveyed breastfeeding policies and practices in health districts in England. All directors of midwifery services were surveyed, with a 93% response rate. An in-depth study was conducted in 8 health districts. The policy of most units was for early mother-infant contact and rooming-in, but observation showed that practices were inconsistent. One obstacle to early contact was the separation of mother and baby for other routine procedures. A policy of demand feeding was reported for 97% of consultant units, but in some night feeding was restricted. Only 30% of units had a "no fluids" policy, the others giving glucose water or formula. The authors concluded that there was a need for wide-ranging discussions on policy, followed by training of staff with a clear explanation of the reasons for changing inappropriate practices.

Cunningham & Segree (1990) compared the breastfeeding knowledge and practices of

7

mothers in a rural and an urban hospital in Jamaica. They found that the rural hospital, with implicit policies supportive of breastfeeding but poor educational resources, had more effect than the urban hospital which had policies that remained unsupportive of breastfeeding (delayed initiation and frequent formula feeding) but better educational resources. They concluded that "...limited resources must be used more efficiently by shifting policy rather than by seeking new technology, programmes or staff."

Stokamer (1990) found that lack of administrative support and supervision caused the failure of a breastfeeding promotion programme in an inner-city hospital in the USA. Training sessions were available to all staff, but attendance was not mandatory and they were poorly attended. Staff compliance with breastfeeding policies was not assessed by supervisors.

Wright et al (1996) describe the experience of trying to change policies and practices in a hospital in the USA between 1990 and 1993. More newborns were breastfed in the first hour of life, fewer received supplementary feeds, and more mothers received guidance in 1993 than in 1990, but the changes were only partial. The obstetrics department did not participate, and gift packs containing formula continued to be distributed. The authors state that "the greatest limitation of the intervention was that it was not a priority for the administrative staff, although they were generally supportive of the efforts of the task force. For this reason, nurses were never required to attend in-service sessions, nor were they accountable for giving formula to infants whose mothers planned to breastfeed exclusively."

In a study of 5 hospitals (2 public and 3 private) in Turkey, Gökçay et al (1997) found that none of them was implementing all 'Ten Steps'. The practice of changing policies according to clients' wishes in private hospitals was identified as a barrier to the support of breastfeeding.

1.5 Policies which discourage or interfere with breastfeeding

Inappropriate policies and practices concerning breastmilk substitutes, bottles and teats can undermine efforts to promote breastfeeding. To become baby-friendly, hospitals are required to comply with relevant sections of the Code and subsequent relevant WHA resolutions. If legislation does not exist at national level, policies are needed at facility level. However, even when breastfeeding policies exist, they may not cover breastmilk substitutes. In a cross-sectional mailed survey of all Canadian hospitals providing maternity care 58% reported that they had a written policy on breastfeeding (Levitt et al, 1996). Only 1.3% reported restricting free samples of formula for mothers at discharge.

Practices which are likely to interfere with breastfeeding, and which are not permitted in baby-friendly facilities include:
- Distribution or display of posters, calendars or any written materials which promote artificial feeding or which include brand names of breastmilk substitutes;
- Distribution of free samples of breastmilk substitutes to pregnant women or breastfeeding mothers in hospital or at discharge;
- Acceptance of free or subsidized supplies of breastmilk substitutes and other products covered by the Code.

8

Any breastmilk substitutes that are required should be purchased through normal procurement channels at not less than 80% of the full price.

Hospital policies related to breastmilk substitutes may be associated with a rapid change in maternal intentions and confidence regarding breastfeeding, even before discharge. Margen et al (1991) studied health facility policies and practices, including the procurement and use of infant formula in 3 Mexican regions. Mothers' intentions and actual breastfeeding practices were also studied, using a longitudinal qualitative and quantitative design. Of 59 facilities surveyed, 80% received all formula free. Only 3% reported purchasing formula at full price. Newborns were fed either glucose water or tea for the first feed, and most were routinely bottle-fed with formula. 66% of facilities reported giving free formula to mothers at discharge. On admission 95% of mothers said they planned to breastfeed at home, 54% exclusively, but while in hospital only 40% breastfed their infants. At discharge, 36% had changed their intentions at admission in various ways, most of them deciding to increase bottle-feeding or add formula, and only 43% planned exclusive breastfeeding. Almost two thirds (64%) of mothers who planned to combine breastfeeding and bottle-feeding thought they would not have enough milk.

A cross-sectional study of the promotion of breastmilk substitutes was conducted in Poland, Bangladesh, Thailand and South Africa (The Interagency Group on Breastfeeding Monitoring, 1997; Taylor, 1998). Mothers who recalled receiving company-associated negative information (i.e. information *understood by a woman* to promote bottle-feeding and/or to discourage breastfeeding) were found to be significantly more likely to bottle-feed their infants than mothers who did not receive such information. The mean age of infants at the time of interview was 2.5-2.8 months. The methods used allowed the results to be representative of the location of the study only.

1.6 Effectiveness of strong policies

A number of reports show the advantages of strong policies, for increasing the effectiveness of interventions. Relucio-Clavano (1981) in the Philippines, Pichaipat et al (1992) in Thailand, and Valdes et al (1993) in Chile, all showed how improved hospital practices can increase breasfeeding. They also describe how, to change practices, it was necessary to change policies, and to ensure awareness and understanding of these policies by medical and nursing staff.

Popkin et al (1991) evaluated a national breastfeeding promotion programme in Honduras conducted between 1982-1988. Hospitals adopted policies of early breastfeeding, rooming-in and the elimination of gifts of formula and bottles for mothers. There was a significant increase in the initiation and duration of breastfeeding, and the authors conclude that changes in hospital policy and training were the most important aspects of the programme.

Bradley & Meme (1992) reported a national breastfeeding promotion programme which started in Kenya in 1983. Attitudes and practices in government hospitals improved, and the duration of breastfeeding in both rural and urban areas had increased in 1989. The principal features of the programme were adoption of a Code of Marketing of Breastmilk Substitutes; Ministry of Health directives to all hospitals to stop the distribution of infant formula and to institute early contact, rooming-in and exclusive breastfeeding; and also training of staff. The policy directives were regarded as a key component in ensuring widespread implementation of the programme.

McDivitt et al (1993) in Jordan evaluated a mass media campaign promoting early initiation of breastfeeding and feeding of colostrum. The campaign was effective in increasing early initiation only among mothers who delivered at home or in hospitals which had a policy favouring the practice. There was no improvement among mothers delivering in hospitals without such a policy.

Heiberg & Helsing (1995) describe three surveys of breastfeeding practices in maternity wards in Norway between 1973 and 1991. Considerable changes had taken place, with early contact, day rooming-in and demand feeding being adopted more readily. Only 16 out of 64 wards had a written breastfeeding policy, and no comparison was made between those with and without one. However, the authors report that "the development of ... a policy is, according to hospitals which have been through the process, very useful and educational."

1.7   Elements of a policy

A specific breastfeeding policy is essential, as changes in general obstetric policies which are not specific for breastfeeding may not improve breastfeeding outcomes. A randomized controlled trial (Waldenström & Nilsson, 1994) found no difference in duration of breastfeeding (exclusive or partial) between highly motivated mothers who received 'birth centre care' (continuity of care, sensitiveness to the needs of the parents and encouragement of parental involvement in care but no specific attention to breastfeeding) and those who received standard obstetric care.

A breastfeeding policy should specify both the need to implement appropriate practices such as rooming-in, and the need to restrict inappropriate practices such as giving infants formula without a medical indication, and using teats and dummies.

The ways to obtain cooperation of senior and administrative staff are many, but generally involve an organizational process such as the establishment of a task force, preferably multi-disciplinary, and holding meetings to reach a consensus. It is advisable to include staff from the mother and child health services as well as representatives from breastfeeding support groups if they exist. Such collaboration may raise awareness of the breastfeeding policy outside the health service and can also be a useful source of information and feedback from the community.

A hospital policy should be written according to the accepted local format, but essential elements to include are:
- general sections on aims and objectives
- any national or international guidelines (such as the Wellstart Model Hospital Policy [Powers, Naylor & Wester, 1994]) which provide the basis of the hospital policy

- national and local data such as breastfeeding rates
- the *Ten Steps to Successful Breastfeeding* and relevant provisions of the Code and subsequent WHA resolutions as minimum recommendations,
- details of practice related to the local situation for each step and the Code,
- technical information and references.

1.8 Process of policy development

Policies may be developed at national level or at facility level. The process is very variable but should include breastfeeding experts and avoid commercial linkages to manufacturers and products under the scope of the Code. It may be adapted facility by facility.

The process of developing a policy is itself educational, and may help to convince staff who are otherwise ambivalent. A policy is necessary to:
- ensure that administrators of maternity facilities and other senior staff agree to implement and enforce practices which support breastfeeding
- internalize the issue among medical and nursing staff
- develop recommendations which are applicable to the specific environment.

The process includes:
- obtaining local data on breastfeeding practices and outcomes, for example through audits
- holding meetings and discussions with all staff concerned
- making presentations of relevant clinical and research results
- holding short courses such as *Promoting breast-feeding in health facilities. A short course for administrators and policy-makers* (WHO, 1996)
- holding study days, with invited speakers
- giving written information about breastfeeding to staff
- looking at other hospitals' policies
- organizing study visits to hospitals with exemplary policies and practices, and exchange of staff.

Coordinating the development of a policy may be the responsibility of one named member of staff or a small committee, designated by the hospital authorities, though authoritative representation from all relevant sectors needs to be included. The policy may need to be drafted by one person or a selected small group of staff members, who then circulate it and revise it until it can be agreed and accepted.

Senior staff and maternity administrators should ensure implementation of the policy through monitoring, supervision and, if necessary, retraining or disciplining of responsible staff. Eregie (1997) found in an African hospital, designated Baby Friendly three years before, that staff continued to give water to newborns and recommend the use of supplements.

Table 1.1. RESULTS OF A CROSS-SECTIONAL STUDY

POLICIES

Country	Population characteristics[a]	Sample size	Exposure	Results		Conclusion
				Exposed	Not exposed	
Bangladesh	Mean age of infants: 2.5 months	N = 385	Company-associated negative information received by mothers	66/76 (86.8%) had ever bottle-fed their infant***	104/309 (33.7%) had ever bottle-fed their infant***	In all 4 countries mothers who received company-associated negative information were more likely to use bottles
Poland	Mean age of infants: 2.8 months	N = 430	Same as above	104/153 (68%) had ever bottle-fed***	71/277 (25.6%) had ever bottle-fed***	
S. Africa	Mean age of infants: 2.6 months	N = 397	Same as above	93/111 (83.8%) had ever bottle-fed***	142/286 (49.7%) had ever bottle-fed***	
Thailand	Mean age of infants: 2.8 months	N = 370	Same as above	47/51 (92.1%) had ever bottle-fed*	253/319 (79.3%) had ever bottle-fed*	

*P<0.05; **P<0.01; ***P<0.001.

[a]: Mothers of infants ≤ 6 months attending randomly selected health facilities

Source: Taylor A (1998) Monitoring the International Code of Marketing of Breastmilk Substitutes: an epidemiological study in four countries. *British medical journal*, 316: 1117-1122.
Cracking the Code. Monitoring the International Code of Breast-milk Substitutes. Country profiles. London, The Interagency Group on Breastfeeding Monitoring. 1997.

Proportion of mothers who ever bottle-fed, if information encouraging bottle-feeding and/or discouraging breastfeeding received or not in four countries

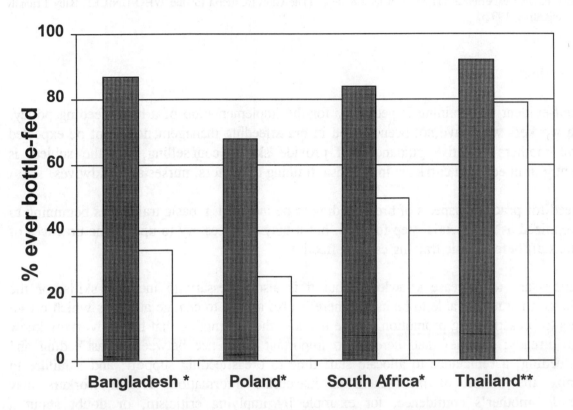

Received information encouraging bottle-feeding

Did not receive information encouraging bottle-feeding

Information received vs Information not received:

*P<0.001; **P<0.05

Adapted from: *Cracking the Code. Monitoring the International Code of Breast-milk Substitutes. Country profiles.* London, The Interagency Group on Breastfeeding Monitoring, 1997.

STEP 2

2.1   "Train all health care staff in skills necessary to implement this policy."

All health care staff who have any contact with mothers, infants and/or children must receive instruction on the implementation of the breastfeeding policy. Training in breastfeeding and lactation management should be given to various types of staff including new employees, it should be at least 18 hours in total with a minimum of 3 hours of supervised clinical experience and cover at least 8 steps. (The Global Criteria for the WHO/UNICEF Baby Friendly Hospital Initiative, 1992).

2.2   Introduction

It is self-evident that training is necessary for the implementation of a breastfeeding policy. Health workers who have not been trained in breastfeeding management cannot be expected to give mothers effective guidance and provide skilled counselling, yet the subject is frequently omitted from curricula in the basic training of doctors, nurses and midwives.

The need for practical aspects of breastfeeding to be included in basic training is beginning to be recognized as an essential step forward, but it may be necessary to update the practices of existing staff before basic training can be effective.

It is necessary to increase knowledge, but it is also necessary to increase skills, or the knowledge may not be able to be used. There is also a need to change attitudes which create barriers to breastfeeding promotion. These include: the assumption that health workers know enough already; a belief that there is no important difference between breastfeeding and bottle-feeding; a reluctance to allocate staff time to breastfeeding support; and a failure to recognize the impact of inconsistent or inaccurate information. Health workers may undermine mother's confidence, for example by implying criticism, or doubt about a mother's milk supply.

For in-service training to be successful it must be mandatory, which requires a strong policy supported by senior staff. If training is voluntary, and senior staff uncommitted, attendance is likely to be poor, and only those whose attitude is already favourable will participate (Winikoff et al, 1987; Stokamer, 1990; Iker & Mogan, 1992).

2.3   Knowledge, attitudes and practices of health care staff

Health worker's lack of knowledge of breastfeeding, and their unhelpful attitudes and practices have been recognized for more than a decade (Lawrence, 1982; Popkin et al, 1985, Lazzaro, Anderson & Auld, 1995). Lawrence (1982) analysed a survey sent to pediatricians, obstetricians, family practitioners and nurses in the United States of America. The response rate was 50% to 75%. One-third of respondents reported that they did not initiate the discussion of breastfeeding with mothers. Over 80% of paediatricians and family practitioners recommended giving supplementary fluids to breastfed infants. Returning to work or resuming studies was regarded by all categories of professionals as a major reason for discontinuation of breastfeeding. Similar results were found recently (Lazzaro, 1995).

Popkin et al (1985) conducted a knowledge, attitudes and practices (KAP) survey of midwives, nurses, physicians and community health workers in a low-income region of the Philippines. Attitudes to breastfeeding were positive in general, but knowledge was poor, particularly about possible "contraindications". Attendance at infant food industry-sponsored conferences in which infant feeding was discussed had negative effects on both breastfeeding knowledge and attitudes.

2.4   Effectiveness of training

Although it is widely accepted that training is needed, only recently has its effectiveness been assessed. Reports can be difficult to interpret because the content or the duration of training are often not described.

Two quasi-experimental studies were identified. Altobelli et al (unpublished document, 1991) studied the effects of a 20-hour breastfeeding course and the provision of standardized educational materials to perinatal health staff in Peru. Three hospitals were included: 2 intervention and one control. The course was attended full-time by 92 and 96 staff respectively from the two intervention hospitals, including paediatricians, obstetricians, midwives, nurses and auxiliaries. 67 and 30 additional staff, respectively, attended part-time. Auxiliary nurses attended an additional 6-hour session of clinical practice on breastfeeding technique and education to mothers. The educational materials focused on 10 messages about the early introduction of water and consisted of a manual for health staff, a flipchart for education to mothers and a take home poster-calendar for mothers.

A KAP survey of all categories of staff 9 months after training showed a remarkable improvement regarding initial mother-infant contact, attachment at the breast, and reduced use of prelacteal feeds and supplements in the hospitals where training had taken place. There was no improvement in the control hospital. Exclusive breastfeeding rates (using a strict definition, see Table 2.1) up to 4 weeks were significantly higher among mothers who delivered in the hospitals where staff had been trained than where they had not.

Westphal et al (1995) studied the effects of a 3-week (133 hours) course in Brazil. 8 maternity hospitals with similar characteristics were randomly assigned to an intervention or a control group. 3 health professionals from each hospital attended the course, which covered all the 'Ten Steps' and devoted one-third of the time to practical activities. The knowledge (measured by pre- and post-course tests) and attitudes (determined using group dynamics) of most attendees toward breastfeeding improved substantially.

Compliance with the 'Ten Steps' was assessed in each hospital before and 6 months after the course, using a set of structured observations, interviews and focus group discussions. Scores in the experimental group were higher after training, and higher than in controls. It was concluded that the course was efficient at improving knowledge, but should include more about strategies for programme implementation, such as a critical analysis of the institutional changes required (see Step 1).

Two KAP studies of health workers before and after training were identified. Popkin et al (1991) evaluated a national breastfeeding promotion programme in Honduras. It took place between 1982 and 1988, and involved changes in hospital policies and training of physicians and nurses. A survey in 1985 showed improved knowledge and attitudes compared with 1982. In 1985 more health workers recommended breastfeeding at birth (87% versus 27%, P<0.001) and breastfeeding on demand (84% versus 38%, P<0.001); more thought that separation after birth is bad for bonding (78% versus 68%, P<0.001) and that a baby with diarrhoea should continue to breastfeed (93% versus 83%, P<0.001). Fewer held the erroneous belief that maternal malnutrition (11% versus 31%), breast abscess (57% versus 77%), tuberculosis (23% versus 31%) or mastitis (27% versus 57%) are contraindications to breastfeeding. National and community surveys in 1981 and 1987 showed a significant increase in the initiation and duration of any breastfeeding.

Bradley & Meme (1992) reported a national breastfeeding promotion programme in Kenya which included training of 800 health workers from all over the country, cessation of free supplies of infant formula to hospitals, and directives recommending early contact, rooming-in and no supplemental feeds. KAP studies of health workers in 1982, before the programme, and in 1989, 6 years after it started, showed substantial improvements. In 1989, 89% of health workers compared with 49% in 1982 advocated rooming-in at all times; 58% (versus 3%) advocated exclusive breastfeeding in the first few days; 70% (versus 36%) knew that breastfed babies feed more frequently than bottle-fed babies; 48% (versus 93%) practiced giving prelacteal feeds; and only 5% (versus 80%) practiced the use of bottles. The number of hospitals reported to practise rooming-in and early contact showed a corresponding increase, while the number using prelacteal glucose and formula feeds decreased.

Becker (1992) reported a small-scale survey of health professionals' knowledge in 3 rural maternity units in Ireland. The unit where breastfeeding rates increased most in 3 years had the highest scores, the greatest number of staff with maximum scores, and the only professional with a postgraduate qualification on breastfeeding. Staff in the other units (where rates had fallen or risen only slightly) felt that they had enough knowledge about breastfeeding to assist mothers. Their main source of information was infant formula manufacturers through regular visits of company representatives, study events on infant feeding supported by companies, and printed information which companies provided for mothers. The author concluded that, in the units studied, health workers needed more breastfeeding education and suggested that a person's own perception of their knowledge may not be a good indication of actual knowledge.

Iker & Mogan (1992) compared the use of bottles, formula and glucose water in a hospital with rooming-in before and after a four-week part-time training programme was implemented. Several training methods were used but there were no practical sessions. Staff attendance was not compulsory or homogeneous. No significant change was found. The authors concluded that providing information alone was insufficient to effect changes in behaviour. Similar results were obtained by Sloper, McKean & Baum (1975) after a seminar with no practical component.

Valdes et al (1995) reported the effects of a 3-day course on the clinical breastfeeding support practices of 100 health professionals in Chile. Topics included the physiology of lactation and lactational infertility, clinical skills, and related policy considerations. Didactic, participative and audio-visual techniques were used. The authors concluded that knowledge and practices improved, but methodological limitations make it difficult to draw clear conclusions.

2.5 Length of training courses

The BFHI criteria recommend that the duration of training should be at least 18 hours, including at least 3 hours of clinical practice. There have been no formal studies of training length, but a great deal of experience has accumulated before and during the BFHI. This generally supports 18 hours as a minimum, though a longer time is often found to be necessary. Armstrong (1990) described the stages in the process of change based on extensive experience of conducting courses in Africa. She found that resistance to the adoption of adequate routines, due to a natural opposition to change and to personal breastfeeding experience, often develops on the second or third day of training. Absorption of new ideas and active planning for change occurs more readily after that stage is passed.

According to verbal reports in one West African country, the BFHI tried to reduce training to 2 days but this was found impossible to implement because the necessary material could not be condensed into such a short time. In countries in Central and Southern Africa, a 5-day training course was said to be essential in situations where no previous training had been conducted. Reports from some countries in other regions suggested that even after a 3-day course further training was required to ensure clinical practices consistent with BFHI criteria.

A controlled study from Brazil (Rea & Venancio, 1998) provides further evidence that the WHO/UNICEF 40-hour *Breastfeeding Counselling: A training course* (WHO, 1993) is effective in improving skills of health workers. 60 health professionals (one per health facility) were randomly allocated to an intervention group (n=20) who attended the course, or a control group (n=40). Qualitative and quantitative methods were used to evaluate the impact on participants' breastfeeding knowledge, skills and attitudes immediately after the course (early post-test) and 3 months later (late post-test).

Indicators measuring knowledge, clinical and counselling skills showed a significant increase in the intervention group in the early post-test, which decreased only slightly in the late post-test. The biggest change was observed in the counselling skills: 'listening and learning', 'non-verbal communication' and 'building confidence and giving support'.

2.6 Conclusions

Cross-sectional studies in both industrialized and developing countries have for long made it clear that health professionals' knowledge, attitudes and practices are often not supportive of breastfeeding. The need for improved training is clear, but it is necessary to learn much more about what constitutes effective, high quality training, including content and methodology, and the necessary hours of teaching and of supervised clinical practice, instead of just the effect of 'any' versus 'no' training.

Improving knowledge may not be effective in changing practices if there is no underlying change of attitude or increase in skills. Experienced trainers often report that a strong practical component can have more effect on both attitudes and skills, than training which consists primarily of theoretical information.

Current experience with the BFHI seems to confirm that 18 hours (3 days) is an appropriate minimum length of training, while longer courses (e.g. 5-6 full time days) with daily clinical sessions are desirable. Training must be compulsory and combined with strong, specific breastfeeding policies to ensure change in hospital practices. Probably neither intervention alone is sufficient.

Table 2.1. COMPARATIVE RESULTS OF EXPERIMENTAL STUDIES

TRAINING

Study	Characteristics Of Trainees	Training	Evaluation/Outcome	Results — Control	Results — Intervention	Conclusion
Altobelli '91 (Peru)	Perinatal health personnel in 2 public hospitals serving low-income families. Int Hosp A: Steps 1, 6, 7, 8, 9 in place (159 trainees). Int Hosp B: Steps 6 and 7 in place (126 trainees). Control (Hosp C): Rooming-in only.	20-hour training + 1 extra day practical training for auxiliary nurses	KAP surveys before (n=323) and 9 months after (n=325) training: Mean age at which HWs would recommend introduction of water	Hosp A (before): 13 weeks; Hosp B (before): 8 weeks; Contr: 2 weeks	Hosp A (after): 24 weeks***; Hosp B (after): 22 weeks***	Improved KAP in A and B after training
			Exclusive BF[a] at 4 weeks	Contr: 13 (12%)	Hosp A: 67 (57%)***; Hosp B: 24 (24%)*	More exclusive BF at 12 weeks in A; up to 4 weeks in B (each vs C)
			Exclusive BF[a] at 12 weeks	Contr: 7 (6%)	Hosp A: 57 (49%)***; Hosp B: 11 (12%)	
Westphal '95 (Brazil)	3-member team from 4 hospitals paired with 4 control hospitals, not previously exposed to BF training	3-week (133-hour) theoretical and practical training course	Compliance with 'Ten Steps': score before/score after training (% increase), data recalculated	Cont 1: 2.2/3.3 (50%); Cont 2: 2.3/1.6(-30%); Cont 3: 2.6/2.8 (8%); Cont 4: 3.9/4.1 (5%)	Int 1: 2.5/3.1 (24%); Int 2: 2.6/4.2 (62%); Int 3: 2.9/4.8 (66%); Int 4: 3.2/3.7 (16%)	Increased compliance with 'Ten Steps' after training
Rea '98 (Brazil)	20 health workers from different health facilities, in same geographical area; 40 professionals selected as controls	2-week (40-hour) breastfeeding counselling course, with 4 practical sessions	Knowledge mean (%) correct scores before course	7.9 (61%)	8.1 (62%)	Knowledge significantly increased and remained high after 3 months with training
			Knowledge mean correct scores (%) immediately/after 3 months	14.4 (55%)***/Not assessed	21.7 (84%)***/20.3 (78%)***	
			'Listening and learning' (SD) mean scores before course	12.9 (3.4)	12.8 (3.2)	'Listening and learning' improved and remained high
			'Listening and learning' mean (SD) scores immediately/after 3 months	12.2 (3.4)***/Not assessed	19.4 (3.7)***/17.9 (1.99)***	
			'Building confidence' mean scores (SD) before course	25.4 (5.3)	26.6 (4.9)	'Building confidence' improved and remained high
			'Building confidence' mean scores (SD) immediately/after 3 months	24.3 (5.9)***/Not assessed	36 (4.9)***/35 (4.3)***	

*P<0.05; **P<0.01; ***P<0.001.

HWs: health workers

BF: breastfeeding

a: less than two servings per week of any liquid in addition to breast milk

Table 2.2. COMPARATIVE RESULTS OF SURVEYS

TRAINING

Study	Characteristics of Trainees	Training	Evaluation/Outcome	Results		Conclusion
				Control	Intervention	
Popkin '91 (Honduras)	Physicians and nurses working in 2 national teaching hospitals, 1 hospital and 1 major health centre	In-service training for hospital staff, and community HWs + Steps 1, 4, 6, 7 and 9	KAP surveys before (n = 338) and 2 years after training (n = 427): Recommend BF at birth: Erroneously believe that breast abscess is contraindication for BF:	27%** 77%**	87%** 57%**	Improved knowledge and attitudes after training
Bradley '92 (Kenya)	Maternity ward health workers in 41 public and 17 private hospitals	Training of health workers and senior staff (time not specified) + MOH policy changes	KAP surveys before (n = 300) and ≤6 years after training (n = 284): HWs advocacy of 24-h rooming-in: HWs practice of using bottles:	49% 80%	89% 5%	Improved KAP after programme including training

*P<0.05; **P<0.01; ***P<0.001.   HWs: health workers   BF: breastfeeding

'Listening and learning skills' of trained and control groups before training and 1 week and 3 months after.

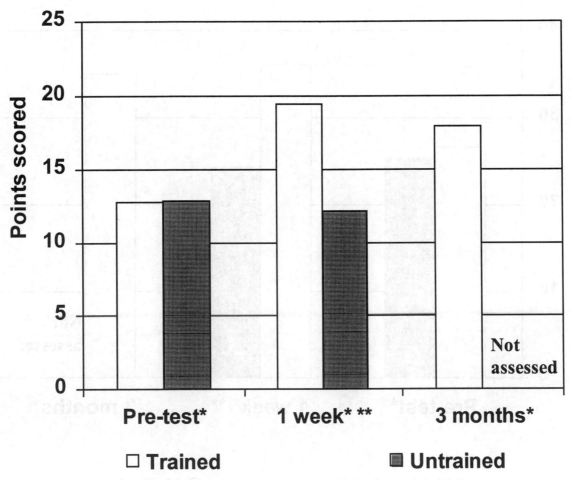

□ Trained　　　　▨ Untrained

*Trained pre-test vs 1 week or 3 months, P<0.001.
**Trained vs Control, P<0.001

Adapted from: Rea M & Venancio SI (1998).

'Building confidence' skills of trained and control groups before training, and 1 week and 3 months after

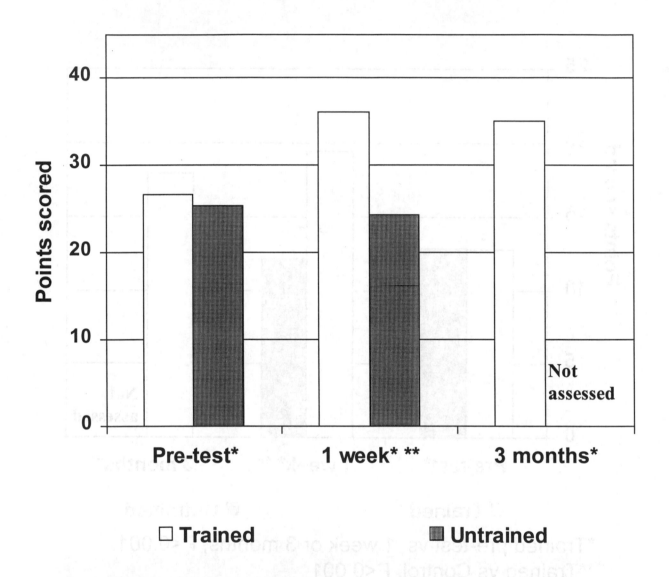

*Trained pre-test vs 1 week or 3 months, P<0.001.
**Trained vs Control, P<0.001.

Adapted from: Rea M & Venancio SI (1998).

STEP 3

3.1 "Inform all pregnant women about the benefits and management of breastfeeding."

If the hospital has an affiliated antenatal clinic or antenatal ward...breastfeeding counseling [should be] given to most pregnant women using those services...The antenatal discussion should cover the importance of exclusive breastfeeding for the first 4-6 months, the benefits of breastfeeding, and basic breastfeeding management...Pregnant women of 32 weeks or more gestation...should confirm that the benefits of breastfeeding have been discussed with them...[including] at least two of the following benefits: Nutritional, protective, bonding, health benefits to the mother...and that they have received no group education on the use of infant formula. They should be able to describe at least two of the following breastfeeding management topics: importance of rooming-in, importance of feeding on demand, how to assure enough milk, and positioning and attachment. (The Global Criteria for the WHO/UNICEF Baby Friendly Hospital Initiative, 1992).

3.2 Introduction

Common sense suggests that it must be important to talk to all pregnant women about infant feeding, to prepare them for this aspect of motherhood. They should be given all the education that they need to make a fully informed decision. However, there have been few studies of the effectiveness of doing so. The step is often difficult to implement, particularly in developing countries where antenatal classes are uncommon. Attendance at antenatal clinics generally may be poor, and women may come late in pregnancy when their infant feeding decision is already made. Clinics may be short staffed and overcrowded, and may lack educational materials.

Antenatal education commonly includes the following components, which need to be considered separately:
1) information about the benefits of breastfeeding, to motivate women to breastfeed;
2) education about breastfeeding technique, to give skills and confidence;
3) physical examination of the breasts and preparation of the nipples.

3.3 Influences on breastfeeding intentions

In many communities where breastfeeding is the norm, women may not need to be motivated to choose to breastfeed – they expect to do so. The main benefit of antenatal preparation is likely to be to help them to breastfeed optimally and to avoid difficulties.

It has been shown repeatedly in developed countries that one third to one half of women decide how they will feed their babies before they are pregnant (Hally et al, 1984; Neifert et al, 1988; Dix, 1991; Graffy, 1992). Their intentions may vary with ethnicity, marital status, and age (Baranowski et al, 1983, Lizarraga et al, 1992) and prior socialization including how a woman was herself fed as a baby (Entwisle, Doering & Reilly, 1982). The attitudes of the male partner, and the pregnant woman's perception of her partner's attitudes toward breastfeeding may also influence her decision (Freed, Fraley & Schanler, 1992 and 1993). Then, around the time of childbirth, important influences include female peers - friends, sisters, relatives (Labbok et al, 1988) – and male partners (Giugliani et al, 1994).

So knowledge is only one of a number of factors which can influence breastfeeding intentions, and it may not have much effect by itself. Kaplowitz & Olson (1983) provided some evidence that printed materials given alone during pregnancy increased women's knowledge, but did not alter maternal attitudes or the incidence or duration of breastfeeding. The authors suggested that a person-to-person approach might be more effective. However, the sample was small and non-representative.

Thus giving mothers information about the benefits of breastfeeding might influence those who have not already made a decision, or those whose decision is not final, but increasing social support may be more effective in enabling women to decide to breastfeed and to carry out their decision. For this it may be necessary to use additional strategies, for example including the woman's partner, mother, close friends or peers in antenatal education programmes.

3.4   Evidence for the benefits of antenatal education

Antenatal education for mothers can increase breastfeeding if it builds their confidence and skills. Classes seem to be particularly effective. A small quasi-experimental study (Wiles, 1984) evaluated the effect of one prenatal breastfeeding class on primiparous women receiving childbirth education. At 1 month, the intervention group (n=20) reported a significantly higher breastfeeding rate than controls (n=20).

Kistin et al (1990) studied the effects of prenatal education on the rates of any breastfeeding in black low-income women who attended a prenatal clinic conducted by midwives. Groups were randomly assigned to attend group classes (n=38) or individual sessions (n=36). A control group (n=56) received neither. A class consisted of a 50- to 80-minute session in which the following topics were discussed: reasons for feeding choice, common myths, physiology, health benefits, common inhibitions or problems with breastfeeding and ways to overcome them. Individual sessions lasted 15 to 30 minutes, and included the same topics.

Significantly more mothers in both intervention groups (45% and 50%) than controls (22%) started breastfeeding. Among mothers who had planned to bottle-feed, 38% of those who attended individual sessions and only 8% of controls eventually did breastfeed (P<0.001). Among mothers who had antenatal plans to breastfeed, 13% of those who attended group classes and one of the controls breastfed for at least 12 weeks (P<0.05). Multivariate analysis was performed, controlling for age, prenatal plans to breastfeed, prior breastfeeding experience, perceived support for breastfeeding, education, gravidity, and employment plans. The chance of breastfeeding during the hospital stay was 4.26 times higher for women receiving any intervention compared with controls (P<0.005) and 5.16 higher for women who attended classes compared with controls (P<0.01).

Jamieson (1994) and Long (1995) have described antenatal breastfeeding workshops implemented in the United Kingdom which focus on knowledge, skills and attitudes (i.e. building mothers' confidence and teaching them how to attach their babies to the breast). An evaluation of the project found that 20% more mothers in the workshop group than in the control group were still breastfeeding at 8 to 12 weeks (Long, 1995).

A quasi-experimental study in Santiago, Chile (Pugin et al, 1996) assessed the effect of a hospital breastfeeding promotion programme with or without specific prenatal education. A pre-intervention group served as the control. The programme included several interventions covering most of the 'Ten Steps' (see Section 11). A subgroup also received prenatal breastfeeding skills education: groups of 5-6 women participated in sessions conducted by a trained nurse-midwife while waiting for their last 3-5 prenatal check-ups.

The topics discussed each time were breast care, benefits for the mother and infant, breastfeeding technique, anatomy and physiology, prevention of problems, rooming-in and immediate contact. A flip chart, a breast model and a baby sized doll were used for practical demonstration. The subgroup who received extra antenatal education had a significantly higher full breastfeeding rate at 6 months than the subgroup who received some antenatal education (80% versus 65% respectively, $P < 0.001$). When women of different parity were considered separately, the differences remained significant only for primipara (94% versus 57%, $P < 0.005$). It was concluded that "prenatal breastfeeding skills group education is an additive, significant, and important component of breastfeeding support, especially among women who have no previous breastfeeding experience." Aspects of the intervention that may have played an important role were group discussion of common myths, inhibitions and problems, and peer support.

Several studies have assessed antenatal care by community-based lay counsellors in developing countries (Burkhalter & Marin, 1991; Alvarado et al, 1996; Davies-Adetugbo, 1996; Morrow et al, 1996) and in the USA (Long et al, 1995). In countries and settings where antenatal visits and classes are uncommon, this alternative may be more feasible. Because they were combined with continuing postnatal care they are discussed in more detail in Step 10.

Education must be made appropriate for the target group, however. Fishman, Evans & Jenks (1988) found that a breastfeeding promotion program in California was inappropriate for an audience of Indochinese women. Focus group discussions elicited the belief that formula was superior to breastmilk for a number of reasons, some related to the Asian humoral medical system, and some to concerns about maintaining weight and energy postpartum. The programme's messages that breastfeeding "is healthier, saves time, promotes weight loss, and helps mothers feel closer to their infants" were based on American perceptions and did not motivate Indochinese women.

3.5   Evidence for the benefits of nipple preparation

Antenatal checks often include breast examination to identify conditions such as inverted nipples which might cause difficulties with breastfeeding. Various forms of nipple preparation are often recommended such as nipple manipulation, application of ointment, and antenatal expression of colostrum (Inch & Garforth, 1989).

Alexander, Grant & Campbell (1992) evaluated the use of breast shells and Hoffman's nipple stretching exercises in 96 nulliparous women between 25 and 35 weeks of pregnancy intending to breastfeed. Women presenting at least one inverted or non-protractile nipple were randomly assigned to one of four groups: breast shells alone, Hoffman's exercises alone, both shells and exercises, and neither shells nor exercises. Their nipples were re-examined after delivery, before the first attempt to breastfeed, and a postal questionnaire was sent for completion six weeks after delivery which received a 100% response rate. Data were analysed according to group allocation, whether the treatment had been complied with or not.

Re-examination revealed that sustained improvement in nipple anatomy was more common in the untreated groups than in the treated groups, but differences were not significant. Women allocated shells were breastfeeding less often at six weeks than women not allocated shells (29% versus 50% respectively, P=0.05). Shells were reported to cause pain, discomfort, skin problems and embarrassment. Five women allocated shells decided not to attempt breastfeeding, 4 of whom gave problems with wearing the shells as the reason. No difference in breastfeeding rates at six weeks was observed between women allocated to exercises or not.

A larger multicentre study, involving 17 centres in the United Kingdom and Canada had similar results (MAIN Trial Collaborative Group, 1994). 463 pregnant women were randomly allocated to one of four groups, of whom 442 (95%) had complete data. As shown in Table 3.2, breastfeeding at 6 weeks was similar with and without shells or exercises. It was concluded that no basis exists for recommending the use of breast shells or Hoffman's exercises as antenatal treatment for inverted or non-protractile nipples, and there is no indication for routine breast examination in pregnancy for this purpose.

It has been suggested that a woman's confidence in breastfeeding can be reduced by antenatal breast examination, especially if inverted or non-protractile nipples are identified (Alexander, Grant & Campbell, 1992). Nipple protractility improves around the time of delivery, and help attaching the baby to the breast in the early postpartum period is likely to be more effective than antenatal interventions.

3.6   Conclusions

There is some evidence that antenatal education is helpful, more for primigravid than multigravid women. Antenatal preparation can have an important effect on breastfeeding, particularly if it covers breastfeeding technique and builds a mother's confidence, so that she will be better enabled to breastfeed.

Group discussions covering topics such as myths and inhibitions, and practical demonstrations seem to be useful methods. Talks about the advantages of breastfeeding are of doubtful value. They might be more effective if those in a woman's social environment who influence her decision to breastfeed are also included - such as the baby's father or grandmother, or close friends.

Antenatal classes may be difficult to implement in settings where resources are scarce. Even where antenatal visits are infrequent, the inclusion of a short discussion on breastfeeding may be beneficial, but specific experimental evidence is not available. The topic most useful to discuss may vary according to the stage of pregnancy: discussing the benefits of breastfeeding may be more effective during the first trimester, while discussing fears and beliefs or having practical demonstrations may be more useful later on. Possible alternatives to health facility-based classes are mother-to-mother support groups, home visits by lay counsellors or community education during pregnancy (see Step 10).

Physical preparation of the breasts, even with non-protractile nipples, has no benefit and is not necessary as a routine.

Table 3.1. COMPARATIVE RESULTS OF EXPERIMENTAL STUDIES

ANTENATAL PREPARATION – EDUCATION

Study [Methodology limitations]	Population characteristics	Control/Intervention	Sample size	Results Control	Results Intervention	Conclusions
Kaplowitz '83 (USA) [8]	Low-income women with 4-6 months pregnancy, without previous successful BF experience	Control: No pamphlets sent Int: 5 pamphlets mailed consecutively to subjects' homes, providing information on BF and bottle-feeding	Contr: 22 Int: 18 N = 40	Knowledge score 4.3 *** Attitude remained unchanged	Knowledge score 6.3*** Attitude toward BF did not improve	Providing information through pamphlets increased knowledge but did not improve attitudes toward BF
Wiles '84 (USA) [8]	Primigravid healthy women (= 32 wks gestation) registered to attend classes, intending to breastfeed; healthy term newborn	Control: childbirth education class Int: prenatal BF education class	Contr: 20 Int: 20 N = 40	6 (30%) in control group still BF at 1 month***	18 (90%) in intervention group still BF at 1 month***	BF at 1 month associated with antenatal class
Kistin '90 (USA) [4] a	Black, urban poor women <24 wks pregnant, intending to breast- or bottle-feed or undecided	Control: same routine care Int I: prenatal BF classes (at least one 50-80 minute session). Int II: one individual 15 to 30-minute contact, topics discussed similar to Int I	Contr: 56 Int I: 38 Int II: 36 N = 130	13 (22%) in control group breastfed in hospital	In group I 17 (45%)* breastfed in hospital In group II 18 (50%)* breastfed in hospital	Antenatal preparation associated with increased initiation of BF
Pugin '96 (Chile) [6]	Middle to upper middle class primigravid and multigravid women, in last trimester, intending to breastfeed	Control: before intervention Int I (BLPP): prenatal and postnatal care (Steps 1-3 + 5-10) Int II (PBSGE): as above + 3-5 prenatal BF education sessions.	Contr: 313 Int I: 363 Int II: 59 N = 735	99 (32%) fully BF at 6 months In group I 235 (65%) fully BF at 6 months	In groups I + II combined, 282 (67%) fully BF at 6 months*** In group II 47 (80%) fully BF at 6 months**	Full BF at 6 months increased with antenatal education, for primiparae and multiparae. Full BF higher with special antenatal care

*P<0.05; **P<0.01; ***P<0.001.   a: Drop-outs analysed separately   BF: breastfeeding

28

Table 3.2. COMPARATIVE RESULTS OF EXPERIMENTAL STUDIES

ANTENATAL PREPARATION – NIPPLE CARE

Study [Methodology limitations]	Population Characteristics	Control/Intervention	Sample Size	Results — Control	Results — Intervention	Conclusions
Alexander '92 (UK) [8]	Primigravid women, 25-35 weeks single pregnancies, with at least 1 inverted or non-protractile nipple	Control: neither breast shells nor Hoffman's exercises. Int: recommendation to use breast shells (BS) and/or Hoffman's exercises (HE). Compliance 63% (BS) and 75% (HE).	Contr: 24 BS: 24 HE: 24 BS+HE: 24 N= 96	24 (50%) mothers not using BS still BF at 6 weeks* 19 (40%) mothers not using HE HE (alone or with BS) still BF at 6 weeks	14 (29%) mothers using BS (alone or with HE) still BF at 6 weeks 19 (40%) mothers using HE (alone or with BS) still BF at 6 weeks	Reduced BF at 6 weeks when breast shells recommended No effect at 6 weeks of Hoffman's exercises
MAIN trial '94 (Canada, UK)	Women with 25-35 weeks single pregnancies, with at least 1 inverted or non-protractile nipple	Control: neither breast shells nor Hoffman's exercises. Int: recommendation to use breast shells (BS) and/or Hoffman's exercises (HE)	Contr: 115 BS: 114 HE: 118 BS+HE: 116 N= 463	104 (45%) without BS still BF at 6 weeks 100 (44%) without HE still BF at 6 weeks	103 (45%) in BS group still BF at 6 weeks 107 (46%) in HE group still BF at 6 weeks	No effect when breast shells or Hoffman's exercises recommended

*P<0.05; **P<0.01; ***P<0.001.

BF: breastfeeding

Step 3 - Antenatal Care

Full breastfeeding at 6 months by type of antenatal care and parity in Santiago, Chile.

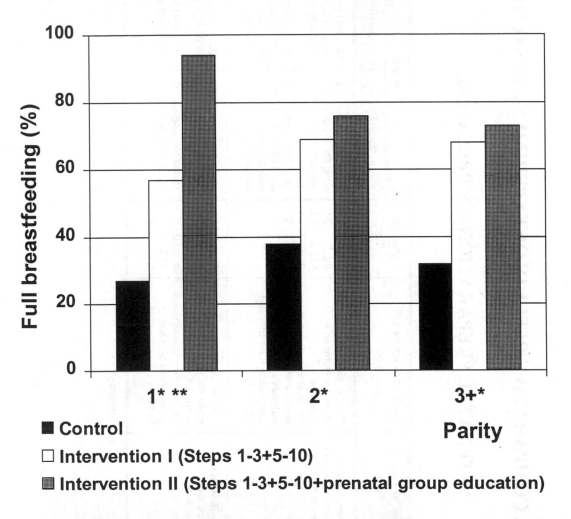

■ Control

□ Intervention I (Steps 1-3+5-10)

▦ Intervention II (Steps 1-3+5-10+prenatal group education)

* Control vs. Intervention I and Intervention II, p<0.0001.

** Intervention I vs Intervention II, p<0.005.

Adapted from: Pugin E et al (1996).

STEP 4

4.1 "Help mothers initiate breastfeeding within a half-hour of birth."

Mothers in the maternity ward who have had normal vaginal deliveries should confirm that within a half-hour of birth they were given their babies to hold with skin contact, for at least 30 minutes, and offered help by a staff member to initiate breastfeeding...At least 50% of mothers who have had caesarean deliveries should confirm that within a half-hour of being able to respond, they were given their babies to hold with skin contact. (The Global Criteria for the WHO/UNICEF Baby Friendly Hospital Initiative, 1992)

4.2 Introduction

Healthy newborn infants are often separated from their mothers after delivery and may not be put to the breast for hours, or sometimes for days, waiting for breastmilk to 'come in'. This can happen with both hospital and home deliveries, in traditional and modern settings. The practice is potentially harmful for both breastfeeding and for the development of the mother-infant relationship often referred to as 'bonding'.

Early skin-to-skin contact and the opportunity to suckle within the first hour or so after birth are both important. Some contact cannot be avoided when attempting a breastfeed but contact itself does not necessarily result in immediate suckling. However, contact and suckling are so closely interrelated that most studies reviewed have used the terms interchangeably, and few researchers (Taylor, Maloni & Brown, 1986; Righard & Alade, 1990; Widström et al, 1990) distinguish clearly between them.

Observations by Widström et al (1987) of 10 newborns and by Righard & Alade (1990) of 38 newborns, have shown that non-sedated infants follow a predictable pattern of prefeeding behaviour when held on the mother's chest immediately after birth, but timing varies widely. Movements started after 12 to 44 minutes, and were followed by spontaneous suckling with good attachment at 27 to 71 minutes. Widström observed that sucking movements reached a peak at 45 minutes which thereafter declined and were absent by two to two and a half hours after birth.

After caesarean section, initiation of breastfeeding may be delayed. The condition of the mother or infant sometimes makes delay unavoidable, but it should not be necessary as a routine. After caesarean section with local anaesthesia, breastfeeding can often be initiated immediately. With general anaesthesia, breastfeeding can be initiated within a few hours, as soon as the mother regains consciuousness (Gonzales, 1990).

4.3 Effect of early contact on breastfeeding

Several randomized and quasi-experimental studies have examined the influence of early postnatal contact on the initiation or continuation of breastfeeding and in some cases on other aspects of mother-infant interaction.

Righard & Alade (1990) studied the effect of early contact on early suckling. They compared two groups of infants assigned (the decision being made by the midwife and mother) to a 'contact' or 'separation' group immediately after birth. The contact group (38 infants) had immediate contact from birth for at least one hour. Twenty-four of them were suckling correctly after a mean of 49 minutes. The separation group (34 infants) started contact immediately after birth, were separated at 20 minutes and returned 20 minutes later. Only 7 of them suckled effectively, the difference being significant (P < 0.001).

Four studies were identified which showed that early contact resulted in a significant increase in breastfeeding rates at 2 to 3 months (Sosa et al, 1976; de Chateau & Wiberg, 1977a; Thomson, Hartsock & Larson, 1979; Ali & Lowry, 1981). One study showed an effect only at one week (Strachan-Lindenberg, Cabrera & Jimenez, 1990) and two studies failed to show a significant effect (Salariya, Easton & Cater, 1978; Taylor et al, 1985)

Sosa et al (1976) studied 40 Guatemalan women who were randomly assigned to an early contact or a control group, and followed up by home visits. Early contact was initiated after delivery of the placenta and episiotomy repair and continued for 45 min. The control group had their first contact 24 hours postpartum. After 3 months, 72% in the early contact group were still breastfeeding and only 42% in the control group. The mean duration of breastfeeding was 196 days in the early contact group and 104 days in the control group (P < 0.05).

De Chateau & Wiberg (1977a) studied 40 primiparae in Sweden. Mothers were randomly assigned to a control group and an intervention group which had "extra contact" (15-20 min suckling and skin-to-skin contact during the first hour after delivery). At 3 months, 58% of mothers in the extra contact group were still breastfeeding compared with 26% in the control group (P < 0.05). Extra contact mothers spent more time kissing and looking *en face* at their infants, while their infants smiled more and cried less.

Thomson, Hartsock & Larson (1979) compared the effect of early contact, initiated 15-30 minutes postpartum and continued for 15-20 minutes, with that of routine contact of less than 5 minutes immediately after birth, resumed after 12-24 hours, in 30 primiparae who intended to breastfeed. At two months postpartum, breastfeeding without milk supplements was more common in the early contact than in the control group (9/15 versus 3/15, P < 0.05).

Ali & Lowry (1981) compared routine contact (starting at around 9 hours) with early contact (45 minutes immediately after delivery, resumed at 9 hours) in 74 Jamaican mothers and babies, randomly assigned to two groups. The rates of full breastfeeding were higher in the early contact than in the routine contact group both at 6 weeks (76% versus 49%, P < 0.02) and 12 weeks postpartum (57% versus 27%, P < 0.05). When interviewed at 12 weeks, early contact mothers were more likely than control mothers to vocalise to them and to rise and follow when their babies were taken from them.

Strachan-Lindenberg, Cabrera & Jimenez (1990) studied the effect of early contact, breastfeeding promotion and rooming-in on the initiation and continuation of breastfeeding in Nicaraguan primiparae (see table 4.1). Mothers were randomly assigned immediately after birth either to a control group with complete separation until discharge at 12-24 hours after delivery; or to an early contact group, with mother-infant contact immediately after birth for 45 minutes followed by complete separation until discharge. Full breastfeeding one week later was significantly commoner in the early contact group than in the control group, but no differences were observed at 4 months. Age was not controlled for, although about half the mothers were adolescents.

A meta-analysis of these seven studies by Perez-Escamilla et al (1994) concluded that early contact had a positive effect on the duration of breast-feeding at 2 to 3 months (P<0.05). However, he cautions that "the effect of size across studies was heterogeneous" and some studies included other interventions (breastfeeding guidance, presence of the father during early contact), which might contribute independently to improve breastfeeding.

A cross-sectional study of 726 primiparous women in the USA (Kurinij & Shiono, 1991) found that mothers were less likely to breastfeed exclusively in hospital if the first feed occurred 7 to 12 hours postpartum or more than 12 hours postpartum (adjusted odds=0.5, 95% CI 0.3-0.8 and adjusted odds=0.2, 95% CI 0.1-0.4 respectively).

4.4   Other outcomes

Contact with the young soon after birth plays an important role in the maintenance of maternal behaviour in mammals, and there is growing evidence that this is true also in humans (Rosenblatt, 1994).

Widström et al (1990) suggested that early touch of the nipple and areola (within 30 minutes) may positively influence the maternal/infant relationship during the first days after birth. A group of mothers (n=32) whose infants touched their nipples left their infants in the nursery for a shorter period and talked more to them than a group (n=25) who were allowed skin-to-skin body contact without nipple touching.

Early suckling can increase postpartum uterine activity and may reduce the risk of postpartum haemorrhage. Chua et al (1994) in Singapore recorded uterine activity in 11 women immediately after delivery of the placenta before, during and after breastfeeding or manual nipple stimulation. The median increase with manual stimulation was 66%, and with breastfeeding was 93%.

Christensson et al (1992) found that newborns who had skin-to-skin contact (n=25), had significantly higher axillary and skin temperatures, higher blood glucose levels at 90 minutes, a more rapid return towards zero of the negative base-excess, and they cried less than babies kept next to their mothers in a cot (n=25).

In a more recent study Christensson et al (1995) tape-recorded crying of newborns in the first 90 minutes after birth. Ten were separated from their mothers in a cot, 12 had skin-to-skin contact for the whole period, and 11 were kept in a cot for 45 minutes and then had skin-to-skin contact for the last 45 minutes. The newborns kept with skin-to-skin contact cried less than those kept in a cot (P<0.001). Those who were kept in a cot for 45 minutes cried less often when they started skin-to-skin contact. The cry was of a special quality, in short pulses, and may be the equivalent of the "separation distress call" observed in other mammals.

4.5 Analgesia during labour and delivery

Analgesics, particularly pethidine (meperidine), given during labour and delivery may interfere with the early development of breastfeeding behaviour, delay the first breastfeed and interfere with breastfeeding long term.

In Righard & Alade's study (1990) a group of mothers had received pethidine during labour. Their infants were less likely to suckle correctly or to suckle at all in the first 2 hours than infants born to mothers who did not receive analgesia (P<0.001).

Nissen et al (1995) studied the breastfeeding behaviour of 44 newborns in the first 2 hours after birth. Rooting by newborns whose mothers did not receive pethidine during labour was more intense and started earlier (P<0.001) than that of newborns whose mothers did receive pethidine. Suckling started later (P<0.05) in infants exposed to pethidine.

A subsample of 13 infants, whose mothers received 100 mg pethidine intramuscularly was further assessed (Nissen et al, 1997). Suckling behaviour was more affected if pethidine was given 1 to 5 hours before delivery, than if it was given 8 to 10 hours before.

Rajan (1994) analysed combined data from a national survey of births in the United Kingdom and a postal questionnaire answered by 1064 women (10% of the initial survey) 6 weeks postpartum. Of women who did not receive pethidine during labour, 45% were fully breastfeeding, while of those who did receive pethidine, only 38% were fully breastfeeding (P=0.01).

Alternative methods of pain relief, to minimize side-effects on both baby and mother, are said to be as effective. Hofmeyr et al (1991) found that the perception of severe pain was significantly lower (58%) in a group of women who had supportive companionship when compared to a group who had routine care (79%, P<0.005). Evidence for the effect of other methods is not available.

4.6 Conclusions

Early contact increases breastfeeding both soon after delivery and 2-3 months later. However, it is difficult to make exact recommendations because the timing and duration of early contact in the various studies is different.

As little as 15-20 minutes of contact in the first hour may be beneficial, while even a 20 minute interruption to contact during the first hour may be detrimental, suggesting a possible "dose response". Spontaneous suckling may not occur until from 45 minutes to 2 hours after birth, but skin-to-skin contact should start as soon as possible after delivery.

Provided the infant is in close contact with its mother and can suckle when it shows signs of readiness, such as suckling movements, there is no justification for forcing it to take the breast. Doing so may have an adverse effect on breastfeeding behaviour subsequently (Widström & Thingström-Paulsson, 1993).

Mothers and infants should not be separated after birth unless there is an unavoidable medical reason. Optimally the infant should be left with the mother continuously from birth, and allowed to attach spontaneously to the breast whenever he shows signs of readiness to do so. An arbitrary but practical minimum recommendation is for skin-to-skin contact to start *within at most* half-an-hour of birth *and to continue for at least* 30 minutes.

Routine use of pethidine should be minimized. If mothers have received pethidine within 5 hours of delivery, their infants are likely to be depressed and may need to continue with skin-to-skin contact longer, before they start breastfeeding.

Early contact including touching of the nipple may have important effects on general maternal behaviour and mother-infant bonding. Skin-to-skin contact may be valuable and should be encouraged for mothers who do not intend to breastfeed, as well as for those who do.

Table 4.1. COMPARATIVE RESULTS OF EXPERIMENTAL STUDIES
EARLY SUCKLING OR EARLY CONTACT

Study [Methodology limitations]	Population characteristics	Control/Intervention	Sample size	Results Control	Results Intervention	Conclusion
Righard '90 (Sweden) [3]	Healthy mothers with uncomplicated pregnancies, healthy newborns	Control: immediate contact for 20 min, separation for 20 min and resumption of contact for 20 min Int: immediate uninterrupted contact for at least 1 h.	Contr: 34 Int: 38 N= 72	7 (20%) suckled correctly at first feed***	24 (63%) suckled correctly at first feed***	Uninterrupted contact during first hour may be beneficial for suckling
Sosa '76 (Guatemala) [8]	Urban poor primiparae, vaginal deliveries	Control: first contact 24 hours after delivery Int: skin-to-skin contact for 45 minutes soon after birth	Contr: 20 Int: 20 N= 40	8 (42%) still BF at 3 months Mean duration 104 days*	14 (72%) still BF at 3 months Mean duration 196 days*	Non significant increase in BF at 3 months (P=0.057); BF duration increased
De Chateau '77a (Sweden) [8]	Urban healthy primiparae, healthy term newborns	Control: restricted contact with dressed infant 30 minutes after delivery Int: 15-20 min suckling and skin-to-skin contact during first hour.	Contr: 19 Int: 21 N= 40	26% still BF at 3 months*	58% still BF at 3 months*	Significant increase in BF at 3 months in early contact group
Salariya '78 (Scotland) [8]	Primiparae intending to breastfeed, healthy term infants	Control I: late contact + 2-hourly BF. Control II: late contact + 4 hourly BF. Int I: contact within 10 minutes of delivery (early contact) + 2-hourly BF. Int II: early contact + 4-hourly BF.	Contr I: 27 Contr II:26 Int I: 29 Int II: 27 N= 109	19 (70%) of Contr I, 14 (54%) of Contr II and 33 (62%) of both still BF at 6 weeks	20 (69%) of Int I, 20 (74%) of Int II and 40 (71%) of both groups combined still BF at 6 weeks	Non significant increase in BF at 6 weeks
Thomson '79 (Canada)	Married primiparae intending to breastfeed, healthy infants	Control: infant wrapped, held <5min by mother. Reunited 12-24 hours later Int: skin-to-skin contact (+ suckling) initiated 15-30 min postpartum, for 15-20 min.	Contr: 15 Int: 15 N= 30	3 (20%) fully BF at 2 months*	9 (60%) fully BF at 2 months*	Early contact group more likely to breastfeed fully at 2 months

*P<0.05; **P<0.01; ***P<0.001.

BF: breastfeeding

Table 4.1 (Cont.). COMPARATIVE RESULTS OF EXPERIMENTAL STUDIES

EARLY SUCKLING OR EARLY CONTACT

Study [Methodology limitations]	Population characteristics	Control/Intervention	Sample Size	Results Control	Results Intervention	Conclusions
Ali '81 (Jamaica)	Urban poor primiparae and multiparae	Control: glimpse immediately after delivery + contact 9 hours later Int: skin-to-skin contact during 45 min soon after birth, contact re-established 9 hours later.	Contr: 37 Int: 37 N = 74	18 (49%) fully BF at 6 weeks* 10 (27%) fully BF at 12 weeks*	28 (76%) fully BF at 6 weeks* 20 (57%) fully BF at 12 weeks*	Full BF at 12 weeks more likely with early contact
Taylor '85 (USA) [1, 4, 7]	White, married, middle-class healthy primiparae, healthy term infants	Control: 2-3 min in mothers arms at 25 min Int I: as above + skin-to-skin contact 30 min after birth during 46 min + suckling Int II: same contact, no suckling	Contr: 39 Int I: 15 Int II: 24 N = 78	22 (56%) controls breastfed in hospital* Int II: 8/16 (50%) still BF at 2 months*	31 (79%) breastfed in hospital (Int I + II)* Int I: 14/15 (93%) still BF at 2 months*	Early contact group more likely to start BF BF at 2 months more likely with early contact + suckling
Strachan-Lindenberg '90 (Nicaragua) [8]	Urban poor healthy primiparae, normal vaginal deliveries	Control I: complete separation + routine BF promotion. Control II: rooming-in + specific BF messages (timing of initial contact not specified). Int: mother-infant contact for 45 min soon after birth, separation thereafter + specific BF messages.	Contr I: 123 Contr II: 116 Int: 136 N = 375	39 (32%) of Contr I ***, and 73 (63%) of Contr II fully BF at 1 week 12(10%) of Contr I; 8(7%) of Contr II fully BF at 4 months	72 (53%) fully BF at 1 week*** (compared to Contr I only) 16 (12%) fully BF at 4 months	Significant increase in full BF at 1 week only when early contact group compared with control I

*P<0.05; **P<0.01; ***P<0.001.

BF: breastfeeding

Table 4.2. COMPARATIVE RESULTS OF EXPERIMENTAL STUDIES

EARLY CONTACT - OTHER OUTCOMES

Study [Methodology limitations]	Population characteristics	Control/Intervention	Sample size	Results Control	Results Intervention	Conclusion
Widström '90 (Sweden)	Primiparae with normal pregnancy, vaginal delivery, healthy term infants	Control: immediate skin-to-skin contact during 45 minutes Int: as above + early touch of areola or suckling within 30 minutes after delivery	Contr: 25 Int: 32 N = 57	Total time newborns left in nursery: 1212 min (580-2070)	Total time newborns left in nursery: 990 min (370-1350)**	Early touch of mother's areola seemed to influence positively early mother-infant relationship
Christensson '92 (Spain)	Healthy term vaginally delivered newborns	Control: infant kept in a cot Int: skin-to-skin contact initiated 10 min after delivery for 80 minutes	Contr: 25 Int: 25 N = 50	Mean axillary temperature at 90 min 36.8°C ** 41 crying episodes observed at 15 min intervals until 90'	Mean axillary temperature at 90 min 37.1°C** 4 crying episodes observed at 15 min intervals until 90'	Early-contact newborns had higher axillary temperature and cried less often than separated newborns
Christensson '95 (Spain)	Healthy term newborns from uncomplicated pregnancies and vaginal deliveries	Control: infant kept in a cot for 90 minutes Int I: skin contact initiated 10 min after delivery for 80 min Int II: infant kept in cot for 45 minutes and then with skin contact for 45 min All: newborn wrapped after birth and placed on mother's abdomen for 30 sec	Contr: 10 Int I: 12 Int II: 11 N = 33	20% of controls cried >840 sec and <1200 sec during 90 min	Int I: 100% cried <420 sec, 80% cried <60 sec*** Int II: 20% cried >540 sec and <840 sec* (I vs II:**)	Newborns cried less during skin-to-skin contact with their mothers; stopped crying when reunited.

*P<0.05; **P<0.01; ***P<0.001

BF: breastfeeding

38

Full breastfeeding at 6 and 12 weeks by timing of first mother-infant contact

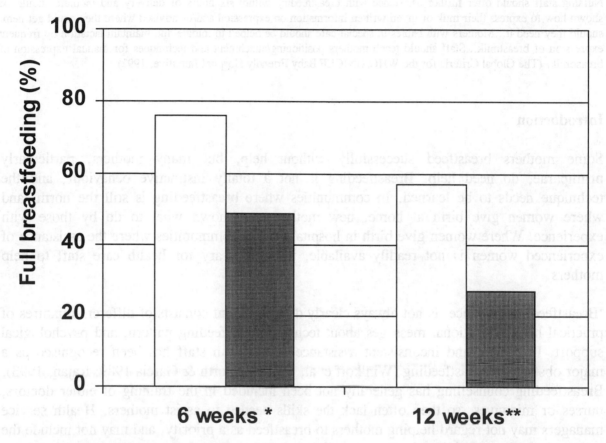

Immediate vs Late Contact: *P<0.02; **P<0.05.

Adapted from: Ali Z & Lowry M (1981).

STEP 5

5.1 **"Show mothers how to breastfeed, and how to maintain lactation even if they should be separated from their infants."**

Nursing staff should offer further assistance with breastfeeding within six hours of delivery and mothers should be shown how to express their milk or given written information on expression and/or advised where they could get help, should they need it...Mothers with babies in special care should be helped to initiate and maintain lactation by frequent expression of breastmilk...Staff should teach mothers positioning/attachment and techniques for manual expression of breastmilk. (The Global Criteria for the WHO/UNICEF Baby Friendly Hospital Initiative, 1992).

5.2 **Introduction**

Some mothers breastfeed successfully without help, but many mothers, particularly primiparae, do need help. Breastfeeding is not a totally instinctive behaviour, and the technique needs to be learned. In communities where breastfeeding is still the norm, and where women give birth at home, new mothers are shown what to do by those with experience. Where women give birth in hospital, and in communities where the assistance of experienced women is not readily available, it is necessary for health care staff to help mothers.

'Breastfeeding guidance' is not always clearly described, but consists of different mixtures of practical help, educational messages about technique and feeding pattern, and psychological support. Inaccurate and inconsistent assistance from health staff has been recognised as a major obstacle to breastfeeding (Winikoff et al, 1986; Garforth & Garcia 1989; Rajan, 1993). Breastfeeding counselling has generally not been included in the training of either doctors, nurses or midwives, so they often lack the skills needed to assist mothers. Health service managers may not regard helping mothers to breastfeed as a priority, and may not include the activity in job descriptions, or allocate staff time to it.

However help soon after delivery has been shown to have lasting benefits, and should therefore be a routine part of maternity care. A mother needs help to ensure that she is able to position and attach her baby at her breast, guidance about how to interpret her baby's behaviour and respond to it, and education about demand (or unrestricted) breastfeeding, and about exclusive breastfeeding. If she has difficulties, she needs skilled help to overcome them. Above all, she needs someone who gives her support and confidence.

Many mothers have periods of separation from their infants because of illness, or employment, for example. All need to be shown how to express breastmilk if it becomes necessary so that the infant can be fed the milk by cup, and lactation maintained. Hand expression is most practical – pumps should not be emphasised, or mothers may become dependent upon them. Routine expression after feeds is not recommended.

5.3   Showing mothers how to breastfeed

Eight experimental or quasi-experimental studies were identified which examine the effect of different kinds of breastfeeding guidance in maternity wards, alone or in combination with other interventions (de Chateau et al, 1977b; Hall, 1978; Jones & West, 1986; Bathija & Anand, 1987; Strachan-Lindenberg, Cabrera & Jimenez, 1990; Altobelli et al, unpublished document, 1991; Righard & Alade, 1992; Perez-Escamilla et al, 1992).

The four earlier studies (de Chateau et al, 1977b; Hall, 1978; Jones & West, 1986; Bathija & Anand, 1987) assessed the combined effects of providing information in hospital and support after discharge. In all four studies, breastfeeding rates increased at 1 to 3 months. The data did not allow a separate analysis of support in hospital alone, though this was clearly a key intervention.

Strachan-Lindenberg, Cabrera & Jimenez (1990) studied 375 Nicaraguan women assigned to receive experimental breastfeeding guidance with either early contact or rooming-in, or to receive routine guidance and remain separated from their infants until discharge. Full breastfeeding at 1 week was significantly higher for both intervention groups. Breastfeeding at 4 months was significantly higher only in the group with breastfeeding guidance and rooming-in combined (see Table 7.1).

In Peru, Altobelli et al (unpublished document, 1991) assessed the effect of ten standardized educational messages intended to reduce the use of 'agüitas' (herbal teas, water) in low-income urban women. Other aspects of the study have been described with Step 2. The educational materials included a flipchart used in hospital, and a poster/calendar to be taken home, both with the same ten messages and accompanying images. The messages were developed using established social marketing methods. No extra practical help with breastfeeding technique was given.

In one intervention hospital, 33% of mothers exposed to one or both educational materials were breastfeeding exclusively at 4 weeks compared with only 16% of those not exposed (P < 0.05). The authors concluded that exposure to a limited number of specially-designed educational messages is very important for the promotion of exclusive breastfeeding.

Righard & Alade (1992) studied the effect of the baby's suckling technique at discharge on breastfeeding duration. Those who were poorly attached ("nipple sucking") were randomly assigned to a group whose attachment remained uncorrected, or to a corrected group. Correction consisted of a 5-10 minute instruction by a nurse. A group with an initially correct attachment was also included. Mothers were followed up by telephone at 2 weeks and 1, 2, 3 and 4 months postpartum.

The incidence of breastfeeding (exclusive and partial) at 1, 2, 3 and 4 months was significantly higher among the groups discharged with correct attachment than in the uncorrected group (P < 0.01), and it was similar in both the corrected and the spontaneously correct groups. Breastfeeding difficulties and milk insufficiency were reported more frequently in the uncorrected than in the corrected or spontaneously correct groups. The authors concluded that the identification and correction of poor attachment helps mothers to

41

breastfeed.

Perez-Escamilla et al (1992) studied the effects of rooming-in with or without breastfeeding guidance. Women delivering in a hospital with rooming-in and a 'no-formula' policy were randomly assigned to a group that received individual breastfeeding guidance or to a group who received routine care. Guidance consisted of practical advice from a hospital nurse trained in breastfeeding management, a breastfeeding brochure and wall posters illustrating attachment techniques as well as messages such as 'breastfeed frequently during the hospital stay'. The nurse had contact with the mother for 15 minutes every 2 hours from 8:00 h to 15:00 h each day until discharge (1.6 days postpartum on average). Up to 4 months, in primiparae, the rate of decline in full and partial breastfeeding was significantly slower in the group who received breastfeeding guidance than in those who did not. No difference was found among multiparae.

Kindness and support even without technical help or promotional messages can build mothers' confidence and have a lasting effect on breastfeeding. Conventional hospital care may have the opposite effect. Hofmeyr et al (1991) in a randomized controlled trial in South Africa assessed the effect of supportive companionship during uncomplicated labour. A group of nulliparous women (n=92) were supported during labour by a volunteer companion, who stayed as continuously as possible and used touch and speech to concentrate primarily on comfort, reassurance and praise. The supporters were drawn from the same community, stayed for at least several hours and in most cases until birth. Their emotional support seemed to be genuine. They did not discuss breastfeeding or help with the first feed. The control group (n=97) received the same clinical care but no support.

At 6 weeks more of the supported than the unsupported mothers were fully breastfeeding (51% versus 29% respectively, P<0.01), they had fewer breastfeeding difficulties (16% versus 63%, P<0.0001), and their feeding intervals were more flexible (81% versus 47%, P<0.0001). Among those who started bottle-feeding, 14% of the supported group and 32% of controls (P<0.01) stated that the main reason was milk insufficiency.

Even a brief individual intervention immediately after delivery can be beneficial. Avoa & Fischer (1990) in Zaire studied the effect of 1 or 2 minutes individual guidance in 304 multiparae and primiparae. Multiple regression analysis controlling for possible confounders showed that the infants of mothers who did not receive guidance lost more weight in hospital (as a percentage of birth weight) than infants of mothers who did receive it.

5.4 Helping mothers who are separated from their infants in hospital

If a mother has had a caesarean section or is ill, or if her baby is ill or low birth weight, breastfeeding is put at risk. Early contact may not be possible, rooming-in may be delayed, and supplementary feeds may be given during the time of separation. However, with good management of breastfeeding, adverse effects can be substantially overcome.

Perez-Escamilla, Maulén-Radovan & Dewey (1996) analysed data collected from 2517 women in the Mexican Demographic and Health Survey (DHS) conducted in 1987. After multivariate analysis, caesarean section was identified as a risk factor for not initiating breasfeeding (odds ratio [OR]= 0.64, 95% confidence interval [CI]= 0.50, 0.82) and for breastfeeding for less than 1 month (OR = 0.58, 95% CI = 0.37, 0.91). Hospital practices at the time of the survey, i.e. prolonged maternal-infant separation and lack of qualified breastfeeding counselling and support, were suggested as the explanation.

Victora et al (1990) suggest that the reasons for performing a caesarean section may have an effect on breastfeeding independently of the surgical intervention itself. In a birth cohort study of mode of delivery of 4912 Brazilian infants, the incidence of breastfeeding was similar after caesarean section and vaginal deliveries. However, caesarean section due to maternal or infant morbidity was associated with significantly shorter breastfeeding duration than when the operation was 'elective'.

The effect of caesarean delivery may be partly due to altered endocrine responses in the mother. Nissen et al (1996) studied the patterns of oxytocin, prolactin and cortisol in primiparae on day 2 after emergency section (n=17) or vaginal delivery (n=20). Mothers who had caesarean sections had no significant rise in prolactin level 20-30 minutes after a breastfeed started, and there was an association between mode of delivery and the infant's age at first breastfeed, and the pattern of oxytocin release. These findings suggest that practices which affect endocrine responses favourably, such as contact with the infant, could be even more important after operative than after normal delivery. Staff commitment to and support for breastfeeding after caesarean section may also be key factors, and may be more important than the exact timing of the first feed, as suggested by two longitudinal studies (Janke, 1988; Kearney, Cronenwett & Reinhardt, 1990).

With low-birth-weight infants, it has been shown that many more can breastfeed effectively than was previously believed (Meier, 1994), some as early as after 32-34 weeks of gestation. However, for many infants, complete or partial feeding with expressed breastmilk is often needed initially. When this is so, adequate technique and frequency of milk expression are necessary to achieve adequate lactation, and eventually to establish breastfeeding.

De Carvalho et al (1985) reported that frequent expression of breastmilk (4 or more times per day) was associated with increased milk production of mothers of premature infants who were unable to breastfeed. There are wide intra- and inter-individual variations in the volume of milk produced at each expression which makes a precise relationship between the frequency of expression and the total daily volume difficult to establish (Hopkinson, Schanler & Garza, 1988). However more frequent expression is usually considered advisable to maintain production. From clinical experience, Meier (1994) recommends expressing breastmilk 8-12 times a day, especially during the first week.

It is important to start expressing breastmilk soon after delivery. Hopkinson, Schanler & Garza (1988) followed 32 healthy mothers who delivered at between 28 and 30 weeks gestation. Mothers started expression on days 2 to 6. Milk volume at 2 weeks was higher (r=0.48, P<0.02) when expression started earlier. From clinical experience, Meier (1994) recommends starting on the first day if possible.

43

A retrospective study in Sweden (Nyqvist & Ewald, 1997) compared 148 infants separated from their mothers and admitted to the Neonatal Intensive Care Unit (NICU), 55% of whom were born by emergency caesarean section, with 3516 infants who were not admitted to the NICU. Exclusive and partial breastfeeding duration was similar in both groups. Early and frequent expression of breastmilk (at least six times per day) was encouraged in the separated group, suggesting that support may have helped to prevent any effects of separation.

Two observational studies by Lang, Lawrence & Orme (1994) indicate that teaching mothers how to express their milk and how to cupfeed their infants can improve eventual breastfeeding of premature or ill infants. (Cupfeeding is discussed further under Step 9.)

5.5   Conclusions

Although carefully worked out educational messages may be beneficial (Altobelli et al, unpublished document, 1991), this may not be the most effective form of assistance. Individual practical help with breastfeeding technique (Righard & Alade, 1992, Perez-Escamilla et al, 1992) and psychological support to build a mother's confidence (Hofmeyr et al, 1991) may be as or more effective in increasing the duration of breastfeeding. The same principles apply when mother and infant are separated. Appropriate help given even during the short time spent in the maternity ward can have an effect lasting up to 4 months.

Every mother needs to learn how to express breastmilk to feed her infant and to maintain lactation in the event of separation. In the case of low-birth-weight infants, eventual breastfeeding may depend on early and effective support with milk expression.

Unadjusted full breastfeeding survival curves of primiparae by maternity ward

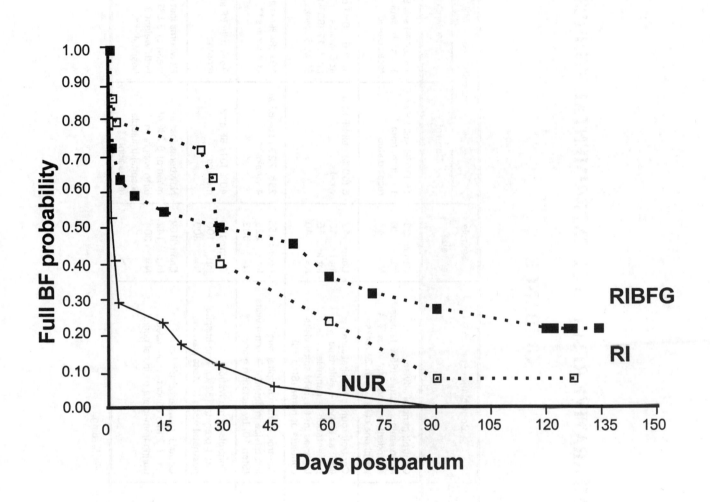

NUR, nursery, n=17; RI, rooming-in, n=15; RIBFG, rooming-in with breastfeeding guidance, n=22. NUR significantly different from RI (p<0.05) and RIBFG (p<0.05).

Reprinted from *Early human development*, 31, Perez-Escamilla et al, Effect of the maternity ward system on the lactation success of low-income urban Mexican women, pp. 25-40, Copyright (1992), with permission from Elsevier Science.

Table 5.1. COMPARATIVE RESULTS OF EXPERIMENTAL STUDIES

GUIDANCE

Study [Methodology limitations]	Population Characteristics	Control/Intervention	Sample size	Results Control	Results Intervention	Conclusion
De Chateau '77b (Sweden)	Primiparae with normal pregnancies and deliveries, healthy term infants	Control: general advice. Intervention: lecture (65% fathers attended) + 3 hospital visits + 4 telephone calls within 2 weeks.	Contr: 23 Int: 20 N = 43	16 (70%) still BF at 1 month, data recalculated	18 (90%) still BF at 1 month, data recalculated	Non significant increase in BF at 1 month
Hall '78 (USA)	Married, middle-class, first-time BF mothers	Control: routine hospital care Int I: as above + slide-tape presentation + pamphlet. Int II: as Int I + in-hospital visits + contacts at home (Step 10)	Contr: 12 Int I: 13 Int II: 15 N = 40	6 (50%) still BF at 6 weeks	Int I: 6 (50%) still BF at 6 weeks Int II: 12 (80%) still BF at 6 weeks	Non significant increase in BF at 6 weeks when personal contact added
Jones '86 (UK)	Primiparae and multiparae intending to BF	Control: routine hospital care Int: advice in hospital + home visits (Step 10) by lactation nurse	Contr: 355 Int: 228 N = 583	256 (72%) still BF at 4 weeks**	191 (84%) still BF at 4 weeks**	Lactation nurse care increased any BF at 4 weeks
Bathija '87 (India) [5, 7, 8]	Educated primiparae and multiparae	Control: no motivation Int: 1 prenatal (82%) + in-hospital + postnatal visits (7 visits planned)	Contr: 100 Int: 100 N = 200	40% fully BF at 3 months	96% fully BF at 3 months	Motivated mothers more likely to fully BF at 3 months
Avoa '90 (Zaire) [8]	Multiparae and primiparae, diverse ethnic origin	Control: routine hospital care Int: 1-2 min education provided during immediate perinatal period	Contr: 162 Int: 142 N = 304	Newborns lost a mean of 6.2% of birth weight in hospital (multiple regression)***	Newborns lost a mean of 3.8% of birth weight in hospital***	Guidance beneficial for newborn weight in hospital

*P<0.05; **P<0.01; ***P<0.001.

BF: breastfeeding.

Table 5.1 (Cont.). COMPARATIVE RESULTS OF EXPERIMENTAL STUDIES

GUIDANCE

Study [Methodology limitations]	Population Characteristics	Control/Intervention	Sample size	Results		Conclusion
				Control	Intervention	
Strachan-Lindenberg '90 (Nicaragua) [8]	Urban poor primiparae with normal deliveries	Control: routine BF promotion + complete separation; Int I: standardized BF promotion messages + early contact (Step 4); Int II: standardized BF promotion + rooming-in (Step 7)	Contr: 123; Int I: 136; Int II: 116; N = 375	39 (32%) fully BF at 1 week***	72 (53%) in Int I, 73 (63%) in Int II fully BF at 1 week***; 68 (50%) in Int I, 71 (61%) in Int II still BF at 4 months	BF messages (combined with other interventions) beneficial at 1 week.
Altobelli '91 (Peru)	Urban poor healthy primiparae and multiparae, public hospital with Steps 2, 6-9 partly established	Control: no exposure to research messages on exclusive BF; Int: exposure to 10 research messages on exclusive BF (talk with flipchart and/or poster/calendar)	Contr: 55; Int: 46; N = 101	16% exclusively BF at 4 weeks*	33% exclusively BF at 4 weeks*	Exposure to messages on exclusive BF beneficial at 4 weeks
Righard '92 (Sweden) [8]	Healthy mothers breastfeeding exclusively at discharge, healthy term newborns	Control: faulty technique uncorrected at discharge. Int I: spontaneous correct BF suckling technique; Int II: correction of suckling technique if faulty at discharge	Contr: 25; Int I: 28; Int II: 29; N = 82	16/25 (64%) still BF at 1 month***; 10/25 (40%) still BF at 4 months**	55/57 (96%) still BF at 1 month***; 42/57 (74%) still BF at 4 months**	Correction of suckling technique increased exclusive BF and partial BF at 4 months
Perez-Escamilla '92 (Mexico)	Urban poor healthy primiparae and multiparae planning to breastfeed, healthy term infants	Control: rooming-in (RI); Intervention (RIBFG): BF guidance (individual practical advice + brochure + posters) + rooming-in.	Contr: 50; Int: 53; N = 103	Primiparae: 3/18 (19%)[a] still BF at 135 days*; Multiparae: 13/32 (41%)[a] still BF at 135 days	Primiparae: 11/24 (47%)[a] still BF at 135 days*; Multiparae: 13/29 (44%)[a] still BF at 135 days	Guidance increased BF rates of primiparae at 135 days
Hofmeyr '91 (South Africa) [8]	Educated low-income urban nulliparous women with uncomplicated deliveries, in a familiar community hospital	Control: routine delivery care; Int: support from volunteer during labour (in most cases until birth) concentrating on comfort, reassurance and praise	Contr: 75; Int: 74; N = 149	22 (29%) fully BF at 6 weeks**; 24 (32%) bottle-fed due to "insufficient milk"***	38 (51%) fully BF at 6 weeks**; 10 (14%) bottle-fed due to "insufficient milk"***	General support increased full BF at 6 weeks

*P<0.05; **P<0.01; ***P<0.001. BF: breastfeeding. [a] : Data recalculated.

Step 6

6.1 "Give newborn infants no food or drink other than breastmilk, unless medically indicated."

For any breastfeeding babies being given food or drink other than breastmilk there should be acceptable medical reasons. No promotion for infant foods or drinks other than breastmilk should be displayed or distributed to mothers, staff, or the facility. (The Global Criteria for the WHO/UNICEF Baby Friendly Hospital Initiative, 1992).

6.2 Introduction

It is common practice in maternity facilities to give formula, glucose water, or plain water to newborns, either before the first breastfeed (prelacteal feeds) or in addition to breastfeeding (supplements). This practice is associated with early termination of breastfeeding. Water and glucose water may be given for a variety of reasons including to reduce jaundice or to prevent hypoglycemia. Formula may be given when an infant is unsettled, sleepy, having difficulty attaching to the breast, or apparently hungry after a breastfeed, or when the mother is ill or wanting to rest, and sometimes for no specified reason.

In many communities, prelacteal feeds of, for example, herbal teas, ghee, or banana are given for ritual purposes (Morse, Jehle & Gamble, 1992). Reasons include the belief that colostrum is harmful, and to clean the infants' gut. The first breastfeed may be delayed for several hours or days, and colostrum may be discarded (Davies-Adetugbo, 1997). When prelacteal feeds are given in health facilities also, the initiation of breastfeeding may be delayed.

Giving prelacteal feeds or supplements increases the risk of infection in the infant. If they are given by bottle, they may interfere with suckling (see Step 9). Giving supplements reduces the frequency of breastfeeding, and hence the amount of nipple stimulation and of breastmilk removed. This contributes in the first few days to engorgement, and later to decreased milk production.

Some hospitals give mothers commercial packs containing free samples of breastmilk substitutes and other items either during pregnancy, or on discharge from the maternity ward. These packs may contain feeding bottles, powdered or concentrated formula, bottles of sterile water, plastic teats, or formula advertisements. Giving free samples makes it more likely that mothers will use artificial feeds, and the practice is not in accordance with the International Code of Marketing of Breast-milk Substitutes.

6.3 Effect of in-hospital prelacteal feeds and supplements on breastfeeding

Regarding the effect of prelacteal feeds (as opposed to supplements) on breastfeeding outcomes, only two studies were identified, and neither was experimental. In a longitudinal study in Israel, Leefsma & Habatsky (1980) found that infants who received one or more prelacteal formula feeds were less likely to be fully breastfeeding at 6 weeks. More prelacteal feeds were associated with a greater likelihood of not breastfeeding.

Perez-Escamilla et al (1996) analyzed retrospectively the 1991/92 Epidemiology and Family Health Survey from Honduras, which included 714 women with children 0 to 6 months old. The use of prelacteal water was negatively associated with exclusive breastfeeding (OR=0.19, 95% CI 0.09-0.41). The use of milk-based prelacteal feeds was negatively associated with exclusive (OR=0.19, 95% CI 0.08-0.43) and any breastfeeding (OR=0.21, 95% CI 0.09-0.48). Water-based prelacteal feeds were associated with delayed initiation (>24 hs) of breastfeeding (P=0.003). The authors concluded that these results "strongly suggest that prelacteal feeds are a risk factor for poor breastfeeding outcomes."

Regarding the use of supplements in hospital, four experimental studies were identified. One of the earliest and most influential was a quasi-experimental study by de Chateau et al (1977b) in Sweden. Infants in the control group (n=119) were test weighed (before and after each breastfeed) and given routine formula supplements. A first intervention group (n=203) was studied immediately after changes were established. They did not receive formula and were not test weighed. More mothers in the control group stopped breastfeeding by two weeks postpartum (45% versus 20%). A second intervention group (n=68) was studied one year after the new routines were well established and staff had accepted them. The mean duration of breastfeeding was significantly longer than in the control group (95 days versus 42 days, P<0.0005). In this second intervention group, because of staff's increased interest and knowledge of breastfeeding techniques, mothers also received more guidance and reassurance than the first group.

A quasi-experimental trial was conducted by Gray-Donald et al (1985) in Montreal, Canada, which looked at the effect of restricting formula supplements on breastfeeding duration. Nurses in one of two nurseries were informed about the new policy of restricted supplementation. Two weeks later mothers were assigned, based on bedspace availability, to this intervention nursery or to the other, control, nursery. In the intervention nursery mothers were awakened at 2 am to breastfeed their babies. Formula supplements were given on special indications such as during the first 24 hours after a caesarean delivery. They were given to 37% of infants. In the control nursery formula supplements were used at the discretion of nursing staff, and were given to 85% of infants. Glucose water was used similarly in both nurseries: 45 mL per infant per day. At 4 and 9 weeks postpartum the percentage of mothers breastfeeding and giving a formula supplement once or less per day was similar in the control and intervention groups (71% versus 68% and 55% versus 54%, respectively). The authors concluded that a need for supplementation may be a marker of initial breastfeeding problems but were unable to say that giving supplements caused discontinuation of breastfeeding.

Nylander et al (1991) conducted a pre- and post-intervention study in a maternity ward in Norway of the effects of earlier, more frequent breastfeeding and elimination of routine supplements. In the post-intervention group, 12% received supplementary human milk and 2% received water; 81% of pre-intervention controls received supplementary formula and 100% received sugar water. One year later data were collected through local health centers. 62% in the intervention group and 52% of controls were traced - losses being mainly due to change of address or loss of records. The mean duration of full breastfeeding was 4.5 (± 1.8) months in the intervention group and 3.5 (± 2.1) months in the control group (P<0.001).

Martin-Calama et al (1997) in a randomized controlled study compared an intervention group of infants receiving only breastmilk during the first 3 days of life (n=87) with a control group who received glucose water *ad libitum* by bottle during the same period (n=83). Mothers were interviewed by telephone at 5 months postpartum. Mothers lost to follow up did not differ from mothers followed up; infants in the intervention group who received only one feed of glucose water remained in that group for the analysis (J. Martin-Calama, personal communication, 1998). The intervention group was significantly less likely to be formula fed at 4 weeks of age than the controls (18% versus 34% respectively, P<0.05). At 16 weeks of age, the intervention group was more likely to continue breastfeeding (67% versus 43% respectively, P<0.01). Most major possible confounders were controlled, except maternal education (J. Martin-Calama, personal communication, 1998).

Supportive evidence for an association between the use of supplements and premature cessation of breastfeeding is provided by three prospective studies. Kurinij et al in the USA (1984) found that infants who received water in hospital were significantly more likely to stop breastfeeding by 4 months than those who did not receive water.

In a prospective observational study of 166 mother-infant pairs in Chicago conducted by Feinstein et al (1986), the use of more than one bottle of formula per day in hospital was associated with decreased breastfeeding at 4, 10 and 16 weeks.

Blomquist et al (1994) studied the feeding routines of 521 newborns in a maternity unit in Sweden and their subsequent feeding patterns. At discharge, 69% of newborns had breastfed exclusively and 31% had received one or more bottles of expressed human milk or formula. At three months, 80% were still breastfeeding fully or partially. After multiple logistic regression analysis the adjusted relative risk (odds ratio, OR) of not being breastfed at three months was 3.9 (95% CI 2.1-7.2) when supplements were used in hospital. In the bivariate analysis a strong interaction was found between in-hospital use of supplements and initial weight loss of 10% birth weight or more. The risk of breastfeeding discontinuation at 3 months was almost 7 times higher with both than with neither of these factors.

However, among infants given supplements for the specific medical indications of maternal diabetes mellitus or gestational diabetes, the duration of breastfeeding was similar to that in the non-supplemented group. In addition, the use of supplements in hospital was associated with an initial weight loss of 10% or more. The authors' explanation for this difference is that "supplementing a newborn on strict 'medical' grounds does not disturb the mother-child interaction and maternal confidence as it does when supplements are given because of 'insufficient amounts' of milk or fussiness". This argument is supported by the interaction found between the use of supplements in hospital and an initial weight loss of 10% or more. In this case, the mother is likely to receive a direct message of 'insufficiency' which may be difficult to overcome.

6.4 Effect of supplements after discharge on breastfeeding

The use of supplements at an early stage after discharge has also been prospectively studied. Martines, Ashworth & Kirkwood (1989) found in Brazil that the relative risk of stopping breastfeeding by 1 month was 3.7 times higher when formula was used at 1 week, than when infants did not receive formula.

Perez-Escamilla et al (1993) studied 165 women in Mexico. After controlling for planned breastfeeding duration, they found that women who were fully breastfeeding at 1 week, were more likely than women who were only partially breastfeeding, to continue for 2 months (OR: 4.6, CI: 1.3-15.8) and 4 months (OR: 4.1, CI: 1.7-10.0). This suggests that introduction of supplements in the first week is a risk factor for early termination of breastfeeding, independent of maternal intentions.

6.5 Other outcomes

Supplements increase the risk of diarrhoea and other infections, such as meningitis and neonatal sepsis, in situations where hygiene is poor (Victora et al, 1987; de Zoysa, Rea & Martines, 1991; Ashraf et al, 1991), and also in conditions with better hygiene (Howie et al, 1990).

Høst (1991) found in a cohort study of 1749 newborns that even a few prelacteal feeds may result in the development of cow's milk intolerance or cow's milk allergy, which becomes symptomatic in later infancy.

Supplements have not proved effective in some situations for which they are advocated. Studies have failed to support the commonly held belief that supplementation with water or glucose water reduces hyperbilirrubinemia of term, breastfed newborns (Verronen et al, 1980; de Carvalho, Hall & Harvey, 1981; Nicoll, Ginsburg & Tripp, 1982; Nylander et al, 1991).

The use of glucose water to prevent hypoglycaemia is not indicated for healthy term infants who are breastfed on demand, even if interfeed intervals are long (Williams, 1997). A chart review conducted by Glover & Sandilands (1990) found that newborns who received glucose water in hospital lost more weight (P<0.03) and stayed in hospital longer (P<0.009) than newborns who did not receive glucose water. Martin-Calama et al (1997) found in a randomized study that infants did not exhibit hypoglycaemic symptoms during the first 48 hours of life whether they received glucose water or not. During the first 48 hours more weight was lost in the non-glucose water group, which was significant statistically but not clinically (5.9% versus 4.9% at 48 hours, P<0.001). At 72 hours no difference in weight loss was found between the 2 groups (4.2% versus 4.3%).

6.6   Effect of commercial samples of breastmilk substitutes on breastfeeding

A longitudinal study in Mexico (Margen et al, 1991) reported a significant association between the distribution of formula samples and the use of formula. When interviewed 2 weeks after discharge, 50% of mothers reported receiving free formula samples at discharge . These numbers did not include mothers from social security facilities who received prescriptions for free formula at discharge. Mothers who received free formula samples at discharge were more likely to use formula at 2 weeks postpartum than mothers who did not receive samples (P<0.05), irrespective of infant feeding intentions at admission. Among mothers initially planning to use formula, 100% were using it if they had received free samples, and only 50% if they had not received free samples. Among mothers initially planning *not* to use formula, 75% were using it if they had received free samples, and 62% if they did not receive samples. The difference remained significant after controlling for maternal age, educational level and plans to return to work.

Perez-Escamilla et al (1994) performed a meta-analysis of six experimental studies (Bergevin, Dougherty & Kramer, 1983; Guthrie et al, 1985; Evans, Lyons & Killien, 1986; Feinstein et al, 1986; Frank et al, 1987; Dungy et al, 1992). Studies compared groups receiving commercial discharge packs which included samples of breastmilk substitutes with groups that received no formula but educational pamphlets, breast pads, breast cream, breast pumps, bottles of water, non-specified materials or nothing at all. Five studies were performed in industrialized countries, one in the Philippines. The rates of full breastfeeding at 1 month and any breastfeeding at 4 months were significantly lower in the groups receiving samples of formula or other breastmilk substitutes. Perez-Escamilla concluded that commercial discharge packs are associated with reduced breastfeeding rates, especially among groups at risk such as primiparae and low-income women in developing countries.

Two more recent experimental studies by Bliss et al (1997) and Dungy et al (1997) do not clearly confirm these conclusions, but they need to be interpreted with caution as they have methodological limitations. Bliss et al followed three groups of mothers randomized by weeks, who received discharge packs with formula and/or a breast pump, and a control group who received neither. Overall duration of any breastfeeding was similar for all groups. However, confounding variables were not controlled for, and prebirth breastfeeding plans differed between groups (P<0.05). Among a subsample of mothers who planned to breastfeed for 6 months or more, full breastfeeding at 6 weeks was more likely (P<0.05) for those who received a breast pump (78%) or only pamphlets (72%) than those who received formula only or formula and a breast pump (64% each). In another subsample of mothers (n=1351) who had not returned to school or work outside the home by 6 weeks full breastfeeding at 6 weeks was also more likely for those receiving only a breast pump or pamphlets and no formula sample.

Dungy et al (1997) followed 725 women randomly assigned to receive a discharge pack containing formula and/or a breast pump. There were no "no item" controls. The rates of full and partial breastfeeding were similar in all the groups during the full 16-week follow-up period. However, the type of breastfeeding before distribution of discharge packs was not mentioned, and mothers lost to follow-up after discharge (n=38) tended to be less educated, unmarried, of lower socioeconomic status and members of minority groups, so the results

52

may not be valid for these high-risk subgroups.

The authors acknowledge that "direct marketing of infant formula products to consumers and the distribution of infant formula samples to pregnant women" is increasing. These marketing practices were not controlled as potential confounders. The effect of giving breast pumps is not necessarily helpful for breastfeeding, especially if feeding bottles are included, which is not clear in this study. The lack of a control group receiving "no item" is thus an important limitation.

6.7   Impact and cost-effectiveness of restricting formula in maternity wards

A three-country study in Brazil, Honduras and Mexico (Horton et al, 1996; TG Sanghvi, unpublished document, 1996) compared 3 hospitals with well-developed programmes and 3 control hospitals in the same cities serving similar populations. Mothers were interviewed at discharge (n=200-400) and followed at one month and again at 2 (Honduras), 3 (Brazil) or 4 months (Mexico) to compare the proportions of exclusive, partial and no breastfeeding as a measure of programme impact on breastfeeding practices. In Brazil and Honduras, the programme hospitals had significantly higher rates of exclusive breastfeeding; in Mexico, the programme hospital had a higher rate of any breastfeeding.

The data on breastfeeding impact were then translated into more generalizable health units, to percentage reduction in diarrhoea mortality, acute respiratory infection (ARI) mortality and diarrhoea morbidity. Disability-adjusted life years (DALYs) were calculated based on death estimates from ARI and diarrhoea.[*]

The costs of breastfeeding promotion activities, mainly programme maintenance costs were calculated and incremental costs (i.e. the difference in costs of activities between programme and control hospitals) were obtained. These costs were combined (separately) with mortality, morbidity and DALY impacts to obtain a set of cost-effectiveness measures. It was found that restricting formula and glucose water and medications during delivery (oxytocic drugs) can be highly cost-effective for preventing cases of diarrhoea, preventing deaths from diarrhoea and gaining DALYs.

By investing US $0.30 to $0.40 per birth annually in a hospital where formula feeding and medications during delivery were still used, diarrhoea cases could be prevented for $0.65-$1.10 per case. Similarly, diarrhoea deaths can be averted for $100 to $200 per death, and DALYs can be gained for $2 to $4 per DALY.

6.8   Conclusions

There are a number of difficulties in obtaining satisfactory evidence about the effect of

---

[*] DALY is an indicator promoted by the World Bank for comparing health interventions. It combines in a single value the number of years lost by premature death and the number of years lived with a disability for a certain group of causes.

supplementary feeds on the success of lactation:

1) It is difficult to assign mother-infant pairs randomly to a "supplemented" or an "unsupplemented" group and to control for the mother's decision about breastfeeding exclusively or not.

2) Some earlier studies did not count water (either plain or with glucose) as an additional fluid, considering only formula as such; their results are therefore only partially applicable (Gray-Donald et al, 1985; de Chateau et al, 1977b).

3) Most studies do not differentiate *what* is given from *how* it is given -- by bottle, cup or spoon (see Step 9).

4) It has sometimes been difficult to change practices consistently. Staff attitudes may not change immediately after new routines are established (de Chateau et al, 1977b) despite training; so "unsupplemented" groups often include a proportion of supplemented infants.

5) Most studies have analyzed together supplements given with and without medical indications; but as Blomquist (1994) points out, the effect of supplements may be different when given for different reasons. Considering both groups together may introduce a bias.

Despite these limitations, it is apparent that the use of supplements without a medical indication is associated with earlier cessation of breastfeeding. It is not clear to what extent the use of supplements is causal, interfering with infants' feeding behaviour, or undermining mothers' confidence; and to what extent it is a marker of mothers with breastfeeding difficulties or of staff with insufficient breastfeeding support skills. Either way, it must be concluded that mothers need skilled help with breastfeeding to prevent or overcome difficulties, so that prelacteal feeds and supplements are not given unless there is a specific medical indication. Restricting the use of these feeds is one of the most cost-effective health interventions identified. There is no justification for giving mothers free samples of breastmilk substitutes before or after delivery.

Table 6.1. COMPARATIVE RESULTS OF EXPERIMENTAL STUDIES

IN-HOSPITAL SUPPLEMENTATION

Study [Methodology limitations]	Population characteristics	Control/Intervention	Sample size	Results		Conclusion
				Control	Intervention	
De Chateau '77b (Sweden)	Urban primiparae and multiparae, healthy newborns	Control: pre-intervention routines Int: no weighing before and after feeds, no 'food' supplements. Studied one year after changes started.	Contr: 119 Int: 68 N = 187	42 days median duration of any BF (median test)***	95 days median duration of any BF(median test) ***	Longer duration of BF when test weighing and 'food' supplements stopped
Gray-Donald '85 (Canada)	Well-baby nurseries, socio-economically and culturally diverse population. Healthy term infants.	Control: four-hourly feedings, formula after BF at nursing staff's discretion Int: training of nursing staff on policy of restricted formula use. Both: Glucose water unrestricted Studied 2 weeks after training	Contr: 393 Int: 388 N = 781	59 (15%) given no formula in hospital*** 278 (71%) fully BF at 4 weeks 215 (55%) fully BF at 9 weeks	244 (63%) given no formula in hospital*** 263 (68%) fully BF at 4 weeks 210 (54%) fully BF at 9 weeks	Use of formula but not glucose water reduced. Full BF unchanged at 4 and 9 weeks
Nylander '91 (Norway) [4 a, 6, 8]	Healthy term babies, birth weight 2500-4500 g	Control: pre-intervention routine care Int: training of staff to avoid routine formula and glucose water + early contact (Step 4) + feeding on demand (Step 8).	Follow-up: Contr: 106 Int: 126 N = 232	Mean duration of full BF: 3.5 ±2.1 months*** 13 (12%) fully BF at 6 months**; 50 (47%) still BF at 9 months**	Mean duration of full BF: 4.5 ±1.8 months*** 28 (22%) fully BF at 6 months**; 78 (62%) still BF at 9 months**	Mean duration of full BF increased from 3.5 to 4.5 months when supplements stopped (+ Steps 4 and 8)
Martin-Calama '97 (Spain) [2, a]	Healthy mothers intending to breastfeed ≥ 3 months, with healthy term infants without medical indications for receiving glucose water	Control: glucose water *ad libitum* from a bottle, after breastfeeds, during first 3 days Int: exclusive BF during first 3 days	Contr: 83 Int: 87 N = 170	At 4 weeks 34% b had introduced formula* At 16 weeks 36 (43%) were still BF**	At 4 weeks 18% b introduced formula* At 16 weeks 58 (67%) were still BF**	Infants receiving glucose water in hospital were less likely to continue BF at 16 weeks

*P<0.05; **P<0.01; ***P<0.001.   a: Drop-outs analysed separately   b: Data recalculated   BF: breastfeeding

Table 6.2. COMPARATIVE RESULTS OF LONGITUDINAL STUDIES

USE OF SUPPLEMENTS

Study	Population Characteristics	Sample size	Exposure	Results Exposed	Results Not exposed	Statistical analysis	Conclusion
Kurinij '84 (USA)	Urban breastfeeding primiparae, normal singleton weighing >2000g. Followed-up for 6 or 7 months.	109	In-hospital use of water	23/40 (58%)[a] BF >4 months	51/69 (74%)[a] BF >4 months	Univariate analysis: NS Multiple logistic regression*	Use of water in hospital associated with shorter BF
			Formula used regularly from discharge to 1 month	8/28 (29%)[a] BF >4 months OR=3.9 (95% CI: 2.3-6.5)	66/81 (81%)[a] BF >4 months	Univariate analysis*** Multiple logistic regression***	Risk of BF discontinuation by 4 mo associated with use of formula during first month
Blomquist '94 (Sweden)	Healthy pre-term and term newborns. Followed-up for 4 months	521	In-hospital use of formula or donor's milk	102/156 (65%) still BF at 3 months OR=3.51 (95% CI: 2.26-5.47) Adjusted OR=3.9 (95% CI:2.1-7.2)	292/336 (87%) still BF at 3 months	Univariate analysis Multiple logistic regression	Use of formula or donor's milk increased risk of BF discontinuation
Martines '89 (Brazil)	Healthy singletons with birth weight >1500g, from low-income urban families, followed-up for 6 months	538	Use of formula at 1 week	RR of stopping BF at 1 month: 3.7 (95% CI: 1.04-13.15)	RR = 1.00	Logistic regression*	Use of formula at 1 week and 3 months increased risk of stopping BF
			Use of formula at 3 months	RR of stopping BF at 6 months: 3.85 (95% CI: 2.34-6.32)	RR = 1.00	Logistic regression***	

*P<0.05; **P<0.01; ***P<0.001.
OR: Odds ratio

[a]: Data recalculated
RR: Relative risk

BF: breastfeeding

56

Table 6.3. IN-HOSPITAL SUPPLEMENTATION: HYPERBILIRUBINAEMIA

Study [Methodology limitations]	Population Characteristics	Control/Intervention	Sample size	Results		Conclusion
				Control	Intervention	
Verronen '80 (Finland) [6]	Healthy newborns without risk of hypoglycaemia	Control (pre-int): no rooming-in, scheduled feeds, supplements. Intervention: rooming-in + BF on demand + avoidance of formula feedings.	Contr: 574 Int: 551 N = 1125	292 (51%) were clinically jaundiced 96/292 (33%) had total bilirubin levels >205 µmol/L	325 (59%) were clinically jaundiced 104/325 (32%) had total bilirubin levels >205 umol/L	Change in feeding routine did not increase risk of hyperbilirubinaemia
De Carvalho '81 (England)	Healthy term breast-fed babies with physiological jaundice.	Control: water ad libitum after each BF Int: exclusive breastfeeding (i.e. no water or other fluids given)	Contr: 120 Int: 55 N = 175	260 µmol mean peak bilirubin in hospital	264 µmol mean peak bilirubin in hospital	Water supplementation did not reduce serum bilirubin
Nicoll '82 (England)	Term breastfed infants with weight between 10th-90th centiles	Control I: water supplements Control II: dextrose water supplements Int: No water or dextrose water supplements	Contr I: 15 Contr II: 17 Int: 17 N = 49	Mean plasma bilirubin on day 6 was 93.5 ± 13.8 µmol/L (Contr I) and 80.8 ± 8.8 (Contr II)	Mean plasma bilirubin on day 6 was 67.7 ± 6.7µmol/L	Supplementation with water or dextrose did not reduce hyperbilirubinaemia

*P<0.05; **P<0.01; ***P<0.001.   BF: breastfeeding

57

Table 6.4. COMPARATIVE RESULTS OF EXPERIMENTAL STUDIES

COMMERCIAL DISCHARGE SAMPLES – META-ANALYSIS

Study [Methodology] [limitations]	Population Characteristics	Commercial discharge samples (CDS)/ No commercial discharge samples(NCDS)	Sample size	Results CDS	Results NCDS	Conclusion
Bergevin '83 (Canada)	Urban educated Caucasian primiparae and multiparae	CDS: given 1 bottle, 1 ready-to-feed formula can, 1 can of formula powder, 1 plastic nipple and 3 pamphlets with formula advertisements. NCDS: no formula sample given	CDS: 212 NCDS: 194 N = 406	165 (78%) still BF at 1 month	163 (84%) still BF at 1 month (P = 0.07)	See Perez-Escamilla '94
Guthrie '85 (Philippines)	Low income, urban women with mean parity of 2.5-3.0. Hospitals A and B	CDS A and B: given 1 can powdered infant formula. NCDS A and B: No formula given	CDS A: 78 NCDS A:56 CDS B: 23 NCDS B:56 N = 213	CDS A: 53 (69%) still BF at 1 month. BF less likely (same data[a])*	NCDS A: 45 (80%) still BF at 1 month. More likely to breastfeed during first 8 months (same data[a])*	See Perez-Escamilla '94
Evans '86 (USA)	Urban, mainly Caucasian high risk obstetric primiparae and multiparae with normal newborns	CDS: given discharge pack with 1 ready-to-use formula bottle, 1 can concentrated formula and 1 can powdered formula. NCDS: given discharge pack with no formula sample	CDS: 55 NCDS: 40 N = 95	36 (65%) partially BF at 1 month; 30 (55%) still BF (1 bottle formula/day) at 1 month	30 (75%) partially BF at 1 month; 23 (58%) still BF (1 bottle formula/day) at 1 month	See Perez-Escamilla '94
Feinstein '86 (USA)	Urban mainly Black primiparae and multiparae intending to breastfeed	CDS: given 1 ready-to feed formula can, 2 bottles of water and 3 educational pamphlets. NCDS: given 2 bottles of water and 3 educational pamphlets. In-hospital use of formula very frequent.	CDS: 76 NCDS: 90 N = 166	64 (84%) still BF at 1 month	79 (88%) still BF at 1 month	See Perez-Escamilla '94

*P<0.05; **P<0.01; ***P<0.001.

[a] Data from hospital A reanalyzed by Perez-Escamilla et al (1994) using survival analysis

BF: breastfeeding

Table 6.4 (Cont.). COMPARATIVE RESULTS OF EXPERIMENTAL STUDIES

COMMERCIAL DISCHARGE SAMPLES – META-ANALYSIS

Study [Methodology limitations]	Population characteristics	Commercial discharge samples (CDS)/ No commercial discharge samples(NCDS)	Sample size	Results CDS	Results NCDS	Conclusion
Frank '87 (USA)	Low income, urban, multiethnic primiparae and multiparae	CDS: given 2 bottles sterile water, 2 nipples and commercial pamphlets NCDS: given breast pads and educational BF pamphlets	CDS: 167 NCDS: 157 N = 324	Mean duration of full BF: 42 days** 92 (55%) still BF at 4 months	Mean duration of full BF: 60 days** 101 (65%) still BF at 4 months*	See Perez-Escamilla '94
Dungy '92 (USA)	Mainly White, middle class, well educated, urban-rural women with healthy newborns	CDS: given formula and non-specified items NCDS: given 1 manual breast pump, breast pads and breast cream	CDS: 44 NCDS: 43 N = 87	Mean duration of full BF: 2.78 weeks*	Mean duration of full BF: 4.18 weeks*	See Perez-Escamilla '94
Perez-Escamilla '94	Meta-analysis of above studies				Full BF at 1 month more likely* Any BF at 4 months more likely*	CDS significantly reduced likelihood of full BF at 1 month and any BF at 4 months

*P<0.05; **P<0.01; ***P<0.001.

BF: breastfeeding

Table 6.5. COMPARATIVE RESULTS OF EXPERIMENTAL STUDIES

COMMERCIAL DISCHARGE SAMPLES

Study [Methodology limitations]	Population characteristics	Commercial discharge samples (CDS)/ No commercial discharge samples(NCDS)	Sample size	Results CDS	Results NCDS	Conclusion
Snell '92 (USA) [2, 8]	Low-income Hispanic breastfeeding women with full term health newborn and who had a telephone	CDS: given formula sample and non-specified items NCDS: not given CDS	CDS: 33 NCDS: 47 N = 80	24 (72%) still BF, 11 (33%) fully, at 3 weeks** 33 (100%) were giving bottles at 3 weeks**	41 (87%) still BF, 32 (68%) fully, at 3 weeks** 35 (75%) were giving bottles at 3 weeks**	Among low income Hispanics, NCDS group less likely to give bottles and more likely to continue BF at 3 weeks
Bliss '97 (USA) [1, 2]	Breastfeeding English-speaking mothers, discharged from low-risk postpartum unit, having access to telephone Subgroup analyzed: mothers intending to breastfeed for at least 6 months (n = 688)	CDS 1: 1 can powdered formula CDS 2: given formula and breast pump NCDS 1: not given formula nor pump NCDS 2: breast pump + manual on use of pump All included breastfeeding pamphlets written by hospital staff	CDS 1: 192 CDS 2: 184 NCDS 1:145 NCDS 2:167 N = 688	Subgroup mothers receiving formula (64%) or formula and breast pump (64%) less likely to be fully BF at 6 weeks**	Mothers receiving breast pump (78%) or nothing (72%) more likely to be fully BF at 6 weeks**	Distribution of formula with or without a breast pump reduced likelihood of fully BF at 6 weeks (major methodological limitations)
Dungy '97 (USA) [2, 4, 5, 8]	Predominantly white, educated, middle-income mothers intending to breastfeed, with healthy term infants	CDS 1: infant formula CDS 2: infant formula + breast pump NCDS: manual breast pump	CDS 1: 240 CDS 2: 245 NCDS: 240 N = 725	18% of CDS 1 group (formula only) and 16% of CDS 2 (formula + breast pump) breastfed fully during the entire 16-week follow-up.	16.7% of NCDS (breast pump only) mothers breastfed fully during the entire 16-week follow-up.	Similar full BF rates during 16-week period in groups of white middle income women who received formula samples, breast pump or both (major limitations)

*P<0.05; **P<0.01; ***P<0.001.

BF: breastfeeding

60

Infants still breastfeeding at 4, 12 and 20 weeks by in-hospital glucose water supplementation practices (*ad libitum* vs. restricted)

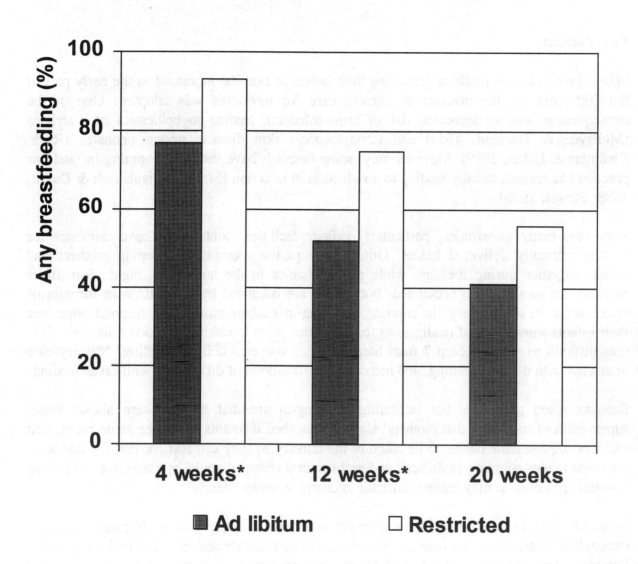

Ad libitum vs Restricted: P<0.05.

Adapted from: Martin-Calama J et al (1997).

STEP 7

7.1 "Practise rooming-in - allow mothers and infants to remain together - 24 hours a day."

Mothers with normal babies (including those born by caesarean section) should stay with them in the same room day and night, except for periods of up to an hour for hospital procedures, from the time they come to their room after delivery (or from when they were able to respond to their babies in the case of caesareans). It should start no later than one hour after normal vaginal deliveries. Normal postpartum mothers should have their babies with them or in cots by their bedside unless separation is indicated. (The Global Criteria for the WHO/UNICEF Baby Friendly Hospital Initiative, 1992).

7.2 Introduction

When the number of mothers delivering their babies in hospital increased in the early part of the 20th century, the practice of nursery care for newborns was adopted. One of the consequences was an increased risk of cross-infection, leading to epidemics of diarrhoea (McBryde & Durham, 1951) and staphylococcal skin disease among neonates (Rush, Chalmers & Enkin, 1989). More recently, some hospitals have instituted rooming-in, and this practice has spread, usually leading to a reduction in infection (Mapata, Djauhariah & Dasril, 1988; Suradi, 1988).

However, many maternities, particularly private facilities, continue to have nurseries for healthy normally delivered babies. Others have partial rooming-in, keeping mothers and infants together during the day, while putting babies in the nursery at night. Sometimes mothers are awakened to breastfeed, but infants are often fed by the staff with formula or water while in the nursery. In contrast, rooming-in enables mothers to respond whenever their infants show signs of readiness to feed, and this helps to establish a good milk flow. It is thus difficult to separate Step 7 from Step 8, which concerns demand feeding. Nursery care interferes with demand feeding, and increases the likelihood of difficulties with breastfeeding.

Reasons often given for not instituting rooming-in are that nursery care allows better supervision of the baby, that mothers' sleep is disturbed if infants are in the same room, that mothers request their babies to be taken to the nursery so they can rest, or that the layout of the ward makes rooming-in difficult and architectural changes would be expensive. In private hospitals rooming-in may make it difficult to charge a nursery fee.

None of these reasons justify the continuation of routine nursery care. Nurseries increase demands on staff time, and restrict interaction between mother and infant, which may hinder bonding; and reduce maternal confidence. Rooming-in is important for all babies and mothers, regardless of how the baby is fed.

7.3 Effect of rooming-in on breastfeeding

Several early prospective and retrospective studies found a strong association between rooming-in and improved breastfeeding outcomes (McBryde & Durham, 1951; Jackson, Wilkin & Auerbach, 1956; Bloom et al, 1982; Elander & Lindberg, 1984). Six experimental or quasi-experimental studies relating specifically to breastfeeding were identified.

Procianoy et al (1983) performed a quasi-experimental study comparing the effects of rooming-in on the breastfeeding intention at discharge in a hospital in Brazil. Mothers were randomly assigned (depending on bedspace availability) to a rooming-in or a nursery group. The mothers' choice of feeding method after discharge was significantly different: 73% of mothers in the rooming-in group and 43% in the nursery group planned to continue breastfeeding (P<0.001). The difference remained significant even after controlling for prenatal care and feeding instructions in hospital. The study did not measure duration of breastfeeding, but it did suggest that rooming-in can affect mothers' attitudes towards breastfeeding, and their maternal feelings and confidence.

Elander & Lindberg (1986) in Sweden studied 29 newborns undergoing phototherapy who were alternately assigned to a separated or a non-separated group staying with their mothers during the day and in most cases during the night also. The non-separated group was more likely to breastfeed during the 12-week follow up period, the difference being significant at 4 weeks (87% versus 50%, P<0.05).

Strachan-Lindenberg, Cabrera & Jimenez, (1990) followed 375 poor urban Nicaraguan primiparae for 4 months. There were several interventions the methodology of which has been described with Step 4. At one week postpartum the percentage of mothers fully breastfeeding was higher in the group who were roomed-in and who received experimental breastfeeding messages (63%), than in the groups who were separated and who received either routine (32%) or experimental breastfeeding messages (53%, P<0.001). At 4 months, the rate of any breastfeeding was higher in the rooming-in and experimental information group (61%) than in the other groups combined (51%, P<0.05).

Perez-Escamilla et al (1992) followed 165 poor urban Mexican women who planned to breastfeed. The methodology has been described with Step 5. The women delivered in 2 hospitals, one with nursery care and one with rooming-in: one subgroup had rooming-in only and another subgroup had rooming-in combined with breastfeeding guidance. Women in the rooming-in hospital were in contact with and breastfed their newborns sooner, spent more time with them, and breastfed more often. Infants in the nursery hospital were fed less glucose water because a policy restricted its use.

Primiparae in both rooming-in subgroups had significantly higher full breastfeeding rates than the nursery group at 1 month postpartum. At 4 months, the difference remained statistically significant only for the subgroup who roomed-in and received guidance. The authors suggest that rooming-in has a short term beneficial effect on breastfeeding, which is only sustained if accompanied by breastfeeding guidance.

Rooming-in can help early breastmilk production. Mapata, Djauhariah & Dasril (1988) in Indonesia studied 414 mothers who chose to room-in or to remain separate from their babies. In the rooming-in group, production of mature breastmilk started earlier (1.85±0.84 days) than in the nursery group (3.07±0.93 days, P<0.001), and clinical jaundice was less frequent (13% versus 26% respectively, P<0.05).

Yamauchi & Yamanouchi (1990) in a review of 204 mothers reported that rooming-in infants breastfed more frequently than nursery infants from days 2 to 7 and that they gained more weight per day. Rooming-in mothers were encouraged to breastfeed on demand.

7.4   Other outcomes

In addition to breastfeeding, the mother-infant relationship may be affected by rooming-in. Even partial (day) rooming-in may be beneficial in this respect.

O'Connor et al (1980) found in a quasi-experimental study more cases of substantial parental abuse or neglect in a group not rooming-in than in a group who roomed-in 8 hours per day, whether they intended to breastfeed or not. Norr et al (1989) found in a population of low-income women in the United States of America that a group who roomed-in with their babies during the day had higher maternal attachment scores at 2 to 3 days than both a pre-rooming-in group and a group who wanted rooming-in but could not have it. Buranasin (1991) found in a retrospective study that the rate of newborn abandonment in hospital per 1000 live births was reduced from 1.8 to 0.1 two years after rooming-in started.

7.5   Validity of reasons for not rooming-in

The reasons given for not rooming-in are not necessarily valid, even for mothers who do not intend to breastfeed. A common concern is that mothers need rest and that if babies room-in at night it will affect their sleep. Waldenström & Swenson (1991) studied the effect of encouraging mothers to room-in at night, when day rooming-in was already practiced. Rooming-in at night did not affect the amount of hours slept or mothers' daytime alertness though they breastfed more frequently at night.

Keefe studied the night-time sleep of mothers (1988) and sleep-wake patterns of newborns (1987) in a group who roomed-in throughout the 24 hours and a nursery group who roomed-in from 7:00 h to 23:00 h. No significant difference in the number of hours slept by the mothers or the quality of their sleep was found between the groups. Seven of the 10 mothers in the nursery group took sleep medication at least once during the 2 nights of the study compared to none in the rooming-in group.

To study newborns a sleep monitor bassinet was used for two consecutive nights after delivery. The nursery environment had greater sound (P<0.01) and light levels at night than the mother's postpartum room. The number of infant crying episodes was greater and the caregivers responded less frequently in the nursery group. Infants who roomed-in spent 33% of the time in quiet sleep compared with 25% in the nursery group (P<0.05).

These results combined suggest that the presence of the newborn infant in the mother's room does not greatly alter maternal sleep, but it improves infants' sleep.

7.6   Effect of co-sleeping on breastfeeding and other outcomes

Night breastfeeding has been associated with co-sleeping (or bedsharing). McKenna, Mosko & Richard (1997) studied the nocturnal behaviour of routinely co-sleeping (n=20) and routinely solitary sleeping (n=15) healthy Latino mother-infant pairs 3 to 4 months postpartum, who exclusively breastfed at night. Routinely co-sleeping infants breastfed three times longer during the night than routinely solitary sleeping infants, suggesting that co-sleeping promotes breastfeeding. The authors also suggested that, by increasing breastfeeding, co-sleeping might be protective against sudden infant death syndrome (SIDS). The evidence for this remains inconclusive. Clements et al (1997) reported from a longitudinal study that co-sleeping was associated with longer breastfeeding duration, even after controlling for confounders.

7.7   Conclusions

Considerable experience has been gained with rooming-in in recent years, and once instituted it is usually reported by staff and mothers to be preferable to nursery care. Common reasons given for not rooming-in, such as that it interferes with mothers' sleep, appear not to be valid. Rooming-in has beneficial effects both on breastfeeding and on the mother-infant relationship. The effect on breastfeeding may be partly because rooming-in facilitates demand feeding. Nursery care makes demand feeding difficult, and rooming-in makes it difficult to restrict feeds. The effect on the mother-infant relationship appears to be independent of the feeding method used.

Infants in nurseries cry more, and their caregivers do not respond as often as mothers who are in the same room. Thus infants whether breastfed or not should room-in with their mothers throughout the 24 hours, unless there is an unavoidable medical reason why they should be cared for in a nursery.

Table 7.1. COMPARATIVE RESULTS OF EXPERIMENTAL STUDIES ROOMING-IN

Study [Methodology limitations]	Population Characteristics	Control/Intervention	Sample size	Results Control	Results Intervention	Conclusion
Procianoy '83 (Brazil) [9]	Urban low-income healthy mothers, no prenatal infant feeding instruction. Healthy term infants, BF at discharge.	Both: initial 5-minute skin contact followed by 6-8 hours separation. Control: one hour contact at each 4-hour interval Int: 24-hour RI, 4-hourly feeds	Contr: 75 Int: 81 N = 156	32 (43%) intended to continue BF on discharge***	59 (73%) intended to continue BF on discharge***	Rooming-in mothers more likely to plan to continue BF
Elander '86 (Sweden) [8]	Healthy term infants with hyperbilirubinemia undergoing phototherapy	Control: Complete separation Int: 24-hour RI + 1-2 hours guidance on infant care	Contr: 14 Int: 15 N = 29	7 (50%)* still BF at 4 weeks[a] 3 (21%) still BF at 12 weeks[a]	13 (87%)* still BF at 4 weeks[a] 8 (53%) still BF at 12 weeks[a]	Rooming-in beneficial (any BF) at 4 weeks
Mapata '88 (Indonesia) [3]	Healthy term infants with normal pregnancies and deliveries	Control: 3-hourly contact for BF Int: RI all the time, demand feeding, skin contact in delivery room.	Contr: 161 Int: 253 N = 414	Breastmilk produced at 3.07 days***	Breastmilk produced at 1.85 days***	Breastmilk produced earlier in rooming-in group
Yamauchi '90 (Japan) [6]	Healthy term breastfed newborns	Control: pre-intervention care, 30 min contact at 3 to 4-hour intervals Int: 24-hour RI + feeding on demand (Step 8)	Contr: 112 Int: 92 N = 204	Breastfeeds on day 6: 7.85 (mean)*** Weight increase (lowest to day 7): 31±15 g/day**	Breastfeeds on day 6: 9.72 (mean)*** Weight increase (lowest to day 7): 39±21g/day**	Increased BF frequency and weight gain with rooming-in
Strachan-Lindenberg '90 (Nicaragua) [8]	Urban low-income healthy primiparae intending to breastfeed, normal deliveries	Control I (pre-int): routine BF messages + separation. Control II (pre-int): specific BF messages + early contact. Int: 24-hour RI + specific messages	Control (I+II): 259 Int: 116 N = 375	111 (43%) fully BF at 1 week*** 131 (51%) still BF at 4 months*	73 (63%) fully BF at 1 week*** 71 (61%) still BF at 4 months*	Rooming-in with specific BF messages beneficial (any BF) at 4 months
Perez-Escamilla '92 (Mexico)	Urban poor healthy primiparae planning to BF, healthy term infants	Control: complete separation, no BF guidance. Int I: 24-hour RI Int II: as Int I + BF guidance.	Contr: 17 Int I: 15 Int II: 22 N = 54	2 (12%)[a] fully BF at 30 days* 0 (0%)[a] fully BF at 90 days*	6 (40%)[a] in Int I and 11 (50%)[a] in Int II fully BF at 30 days* (II vs C) 1 (8%)[a] in Int I and 6 (27%)[a] in Int II fully BF at 90 days* (II vs C)	Full BF increased up to 90 days with rooming-in and BF guidance for primiparae

*P<0.05; **P<0.01; ***P<0.001.   RI: Rooming-in   [a]: Data recalculated   BF: breastfeeding

66

Table 7.2. COMPARATIVE RESULTS OF EXPERIMENTAL STUDIES
ROOMING-IN – OTHER OUTCOMES

Study [Methodology limitations]	Population characteristics	Control/Intervention	Sample size	Results Control	Results Intervention	Conclusion
O'Connor '80 (USA)	Healthy low-income primiparae with healthy newborns	Control: contact after 12 hours, only for feeding Int: contact after 7-21 hours, rooming-in 11.4 h during first 48 hours (mean)	Contr: 158 Int: 143 N = 301	9 cases of substantial parental abuse or neglect during 17 months*	1 case of substantial parental abuse or neglect during 17 months*	Mothers rooming-in (partially) less likely to develop parenting abuse or neglect
Norr '89 (USA) [6]	Medically indigent primiparae with normal delivery and healthy term infants, most bottle-feeding	Control I: 45-min contact four times/day, pre-intervention Control II: same as above, despite maternal desire to room-in Intervention: day rooming-in.	Contr I: 72 Contr II: 35 Int: 77 N = 184	Maternal attachment score on day 2-3: Contr I: 82.2 ± 21 (mean ± SD)* Contr II: 80.2 ± 19.9	Maternal attachment score on day 2-3: 88.9 ± 21 (mean ± SD)*	Mothers rooming-in more attached to babies
Keefe '87 and '88 (USA) [3]	Multiparae with normal deliveries, term low-risk breastfed infants	Control: rooming-in from 7 h to 23 h Int: as above + night rooming-in.	Contr: 10 Int: 11 N = 21	Maternal sleep per 8-hour period on nights 1-2: 5.35 h Infant's crib time in quiet sleep: 25%* Infant's in-crib mean crying time/night: 20.8 min***	Maternal sleep per 8-hour period on nights 1-2: 5.55 h Infant's crib time spent in quiet sleep: 33%* Infant's mean crying time/night: 1.4 min***	Night rooming-in did not reduce maternal sleep; infants had more quiet sleep and cried less time
Waldenstrom '91 (Sweden) [6]	Normal delivery, healthy baby	Control (pre-int): rooming-in from 6 h to 22 h Int: as above + encouragement for rooming-in at night (staff training, antenatal information).	Contr: 104 Int: 111 N = 215	1.5 breastfeeds on night 3 (mean)* 5.7 hours slept by mother on day 3 (mean)	1.8 breastfeeds on night 3 (mean)* 5.6 hours slept by mother on day 3 (mean)	Night rooming-in did not reduce maternal sleep, slightly more breastfeeds on night 3

*P<0.05; **P<0.01; ***P<0.001.

RI: Rooming-in

BF: breastfeeding

STEP 8

8.1 "Encourage breastfeeding on demand."

Mothers of normal babies (including caesareans) who are breastfeeding should have no restrictions placed on the frequency or length of their babies' breastfeeds. They should be advised to breastfeed their babies whenever they are hungry or as often as the baby wants and they should wake their babies for breastfeeding if the babies sleep too long or the mother's breasts are overfull. (The Global Criteria for the WHO/UNICEF Baby Friendly Hospital Initiative, 1992).

8.2 Introduction

The idea that fixed breastfeeding schedules are better for both the infant and the mother was introduced at the beginning of the 20th century in an attempt to make infant feeding 'scientific' and safe (Fisher, 1985; Klaus, 1987; Inch & Garforth, 1989). On purely theoretical grounds, it was supposed that the infant's stomach needed a certain interval (3 to 4 hours) to be emptied, that night feeds had to be avoided, and that prolonged feeds caused diarrhoea, vomiting, failure to thrive and sore nipples. These ideas still prevail in some places. More generally it is now accepted that scheduling feeds leads to breastfeeding problems and insufficient milk production which may cause mothers to start artificial feeding. Restricting feed length may result in the baby getting less of the energy rich hindmilk (Woolridge & Baum, 1993).

There may still, however, be a gap between policy and practice. Demand feeding may be specified but staff may suggest "teaching" the newborn a schedule before he/she leaves the hospital (Garforth & Garcia, 1989) or they may recommend starting with short feeds to prevent sore nipples.

With demand feeding (also known as 'unrestricted', or 'baby led' or 'in response to the baby's cues'), the frequency and length of feeds varies both between infants and from day to day. Many infants feed every 2 to 3 hours or more often, with some longer interfeed intervals. The total number of feeds each day is usually more than the 6 to 8 allowed by a traditional hospital schedule.

In hospital, truly unrestricted feeding is only possible with 24-hour rooming-in, which enables the mother to respond when her infant shows readiness to feed. Thus it is difficult to assess the effect of demand feeding independently of Step 7.

8.3 Frequency and length of suckling soon after birth

The delivery of the placenta results in a fall in the levels of oestrogen and progesterone in the mother's blood, which allows prolactin to operate on the mammary gland and to start the production of milk. The amount of milk produced is then adapted during the first few weeks to the infant's needs, partly by the prolactin which is secreted in response to suckling, and partly by the local effects on the gland of the removal of milk, both being largely determined by the infant's appetite (Woolridge & Baum, 1993; Wilde, Prentice & Peaker, 1995; Hartmann et al, 1996). Asking mothers to restrict either the frequency or the length of breastfeeds can interfere with the adaptation process, and may lead to engorgement, insufficiency of milk production, and other problems.

When there are no restrictions, the frequency and length of breastfeeds varies widely. Howie et al (1981) observed 50 mothers during 2 consecutive breastfeeds, at 5-7 days postpartum. The length of feeds varied between 7 and 30 min, the initial rate of milk flow varied from 1 to 14 g/min, and the final milk intake from 42 to 125 g per feed. De Carvalho et al (1982a) in the United States studied 46 mother-infant pairs breastfeeding on demand, without supplements. The suckling frequency varied during the first two weeks of life from 6.5 to 16.5 feeds/24 h, and at one month from 5 to 11 feeds/24 h. The mean total daily suckling time was 86 to 304 and 75 to 405 min/24 h in the first two weeks and at one month of age, respectively. The daily milk intake at 1 month ranged from 395 to 1011 ml, and was not correlated with the frequency or duration of suckling.

Feeding 10-15 times a day is not unusual. Diaz et al (1995) followed 1217 healthy Chilean mothers breastfeeding on demand, and reported that the suckling frequency at 1 month was 8.0 ± 2.7 feeds during the day and 3.5 ± 2.2 feeds at night. At 6 months, suckling frequency was 7.7 ± 2.7 and 2.6 ± 1.7 respectively.

8.4 The effect of unrestricted breastfeeding

Four quasi-experimental studies of the effect of unrestricted breastfeeding were identified (Illingworth & Stone, 1952; Slaven & Harvey, 1981; de Carvalho et al, 1983 and 1984). One study (Salariya, Easton & Cater, 1978) compared the effect of 2-hourly feeds versus 4-hourly feeds but differences did not reach significance.

Illingworth & Stone (1952) compared the weight gain and the incidence of full breastfeeding in infants randomly allocated to different maternity wards. In one ward, 106 infants were fed on a fixed schedule (4-hourly feeds, six times per day). In another ward 131 babies were fed on demand.

Demand feeding started on day 3. The mean number of feeds in the demand fed group was 6.4 per 24 hours. By the ninth day 49% of demand fed infants had regained their birth weight compared to 36% on the fixed schedule. Significantly more mothers on the fixed schedule had sore nipples (27% versus 13%) and 'overdistension' or engorged breasts ((34% versus 17%). At one month more demand fed babies were fully breastfed (80% compared with 65%).

Slaven & Harvey (1981) studied the effect of restricted length of feeds, when feed frequency was 'on demand'. An intervention group was instructed to feed "for any length of time that seemed suitable to them". A control group was instructed to feed for 3 minutes on each breast on postpartum day 1; 5 minutes on day 2; 7 minutes on day 3; and 10 minutes thereafter. At 6 weeks the proportion of mothers still breastfeeding was significantly higher in the unlimited suckling group than in the timed suckling group ($P < 0.0005$). Nipple soreness and breast engorgement did not differ between the groups.

De Carvalho et al (1983) followed for 35 days a control group of mothers assigned to a fixed schedule and an experimental group assigned to demand feeding. On day 15 the milk intake of the experimental group was significantly higher (725 ml versus 502 ml/24 h, P<0.0002) and infants had gained more weight from birth (561 versus 347 g, P<0.02). However, milk intake and weight gain were not significantly different on day 35 and subsequent follow-up was unhelpful owing to high attrition rates.

De Carvalho et al (1984) also compared nipple soreness reported by 17 mothers in a control group (fixed schedule) and 15 mothers in an experimental group (demand feeding) followed until day 10 postpartum. The number of feeds was significantly higher in the experimental group than in the control group (10 versus 7.4 feedings/24 h, P<0.0001). Nipple soreness did not increase with longer or more frequent breastfeeds.

In a prospective cohort study of urban poor Brazilian infants under 6 months of age (Martines, Ashworth & Kirkwood, 1989) it was found that frequent breastfeeding after discharge from the maternity (more than 6 times/day at one month) was associated with longer duration of breastfeeding than feeding on a fixed schedule. Even after controlling for mixed breast and bottle-feeding, the effect of frequent breastfeeds remained significant at 3 to 6 months.

8.5   Other outcomes

As discussed with Step 6, increased fluids are often recommended for treatment of physiological jaundice. Glucose water supplements are not effective, but more frequent breastfeeding apparently is. De Carvalho (1982b) found a significant association between frequent breastfeeding in hospital (more than 8 times per 24 hours) during the first 3 days of life and lower serum bilirubin levels on day 3 (P<0.01), though weight loss was similar regardless of breastfeeding frequency.

Yamauchi & Yamanouchi, in a prospective study of 140 infants (1990) found that higher feeding frequency during the first postpartum day was strongly correlated with reduced hyperbilirubinemia on day 6. Higher feeding frequency was also strongly correlated with increased breastmilk intake on days 3 and 5 (P<0.05) and a decrease in weight loss from birth to day 7 (P<0.01).

8.6   Conclusions

The breastfeeding pattern, that is the number of episodes and the total duration of suckling per 24 hours, varies widely between mother-infant pairs and over time, so truly unrestricted breastfeeding cannot follow guidelines based on mean values.

Breastfeeding on demand has clear benefits. Fears of possible harmful effects, such as the increasing risk of sore nipples, are groundless. It is now known that sore nipples are mainly due to poor attachment at the breast, unrelated to duration of suckling (Woolridge, 1986b).

The benefits of demand feeding for the infant include less weight loss in the immediate postpartum period and increased duration of breastfeeding subsequently. Frequent feeding is associated with less hyperbilirubinemia during the early neonatal period. For mothers, demand feeding helps to prevent engorgement, and breastfeeding is established more easily. Reports of experience from hospitals after demand feeding has been introduced often confirm that engorgement and associated problems become much less common, though these observations have seldom been formally recorded. Few maternity staff who have witnessed the transition are willing to return to feeding on a fixed schedule, with the associated need for comforting crying babies while they wait for feeding time, and the frustration of trying to attach a frantic baby to the engorged breast of a distressed mother.

Table 8.1. COMPARATIVE RESULTS OF EXPERIMENTAL STUDIES

DEMAND FEEDING

Study [Methodology limitations]	Population characteristics	Control/Intervention	Sample size	Results Control	Results Intervention	Conclusion
Illingworth '52 (England) [2]	Healthy term infants	Control: fed four-hourly Int: demand BF after day 2. Both: 24-hour rooming-in	Contr: 96 Int: 122 N = 218	62 (64.5%) fully BF at 1 month**	98 (80.3%) fully BF at 1 month**	Demand feeding seemed beneficial (full BF) at 1 month
Salariya '78 (Scotland) [8]	Primiparous mothers intending to breastfeed, healthy term infants	Control I: 4-hourly BF + early contact Control II: 4 hourly BF + late contact Int I: 2-hourly BF + early contact Int II: 2-hourly BF + late contact.	Contr I: 27 Contr II:26 Int I: 29 Int II: 27 N = 109	Still BF at 6 weeks: 20 (74%) in Cont I 14 (54%) in Cont II 34 (64%) In Cont I+II	Still BF at 6 weeks: 20 (69%) in Int I 19 (70%) in Int II 39 (70%) in Int I+II	Non significant increase in BF at 6 weeks when infants fed 2-hourly
Slaven '81 (England) [2]	Primiparae and multiparae intending to breastfeed, who had a telephone at home	Control: restricted duration of feed on each breast (3, 5, 7 and 10 minutes from days 1 to 4, 10 min thereafter) Int: unlimited suckling time Both: unlimited frequency of breastfeeds	Contr: 100 Int: 100 N = 200	57% still BF at 6 weeks*** 37% reported engorged breasts, 33% reported sore nipples	80% still BF at 6 weeks*** 27% reported engorged breasts, 38% reported sore nipples	Mothers demand feeding more likely to continue BF, similar proportion of breast engorgement and nipple soreness
De Carvalho '83 (USA) [1, 4]	Urban mothers with normal delivery, planning to breastfeed, term infants.	Control(pre-int): 3-4 hourly BF Int: instruction to feed whenever infant seemed hungry Both: one BF class in hospital including basic breast care techniques	Contr: 24 Int: 20 N = 44	Mean feedings/24 hrs (days 1-14): 7.3±1.4 Infant weight gain to day 15: 347 g* Milk intake on day 15: 502 ml/24 hrs***	Mean feedings/24 hrs (days 1-14): 9.9±1.9*** Infant weight gain to day 15: 561 g* Milk intake on day 15: 725 ml/24 hrs***	Demand feeding seemed beneficial for feeding frequency, weight gain and milk intake on day 15
De Carvalho '84 (USA)	Mothers with uncomplicated term gestation and normal delivery, fully BF	Control (pre-int): 3-4 hourly BF Int: BF whenever infant fussy, sucking fingers or with mouthing movements Both: 1 BF class, no water or formula	Contr: 17 Int: 15 N = 32	7.7±1.4 feeds/day (days 6-10)*** Nipple soreness score: 0.75±0.73 points (days 6-10)	10±2.3 feeds/day (days 6-10)*** Nipple soreness score: 0.44±0.5 points (days 6-10)	Mothers demand feeding breastfed more frequently but did not differ in nipple soreness reports

*P<0.05; **P<0.01; ***P<0.001.

Proportion of infants fully breastfeeding on discharge and at 1 month of age, by breastfeeding pattern in the maternity unit

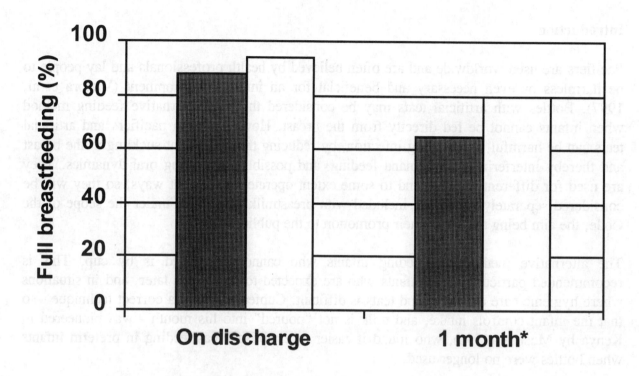

■ Rigid schedule   □ Feeding on demand

*Rigid schedule vs Feeding on demand: P<0.01.

Adapted from: Illingworth RS & Stone DGH (1952).

STEP 9

9.1 "Give no artificial teats or pacifiers (also called dummies or soothers) to breast-feeding infants."

Infants should not be fed using bottles with artificial teats (nipples) nor allowed to suck on pacifiers. (The Global Criteria for the WHO/UNICEF Baby Friendly Hospital Initiative, 1992).

9.2 Introduction

Pacifiers are used worldwide and are often believed by health professionals and lay people to be harmless or even necessary and beneficial for an infant's development (Victora et al, 1997). Bottles with artificial teats may be considered the only alternative feeding method when infants cannot be fed directly from the breast. However, both pacifiers and artificial teats can be harmful, by carrying infection, by reducing the time spent suckling at the breast and thereby interfering with demand feeding, and possibly by altering oral dynamics. They are used for different reasons, and to some extent operate in different ways, so they will be considered separately. Teats are included with breastmilk substitutes under the scope of the Code, the aim being to restrict their promotion to the public.

The alternative method for feeding infants who cannot breastfeed is by cup. This is recommended particularly for infants who are expected to breastfeed later, and in situations where hygienic care of bottles and teats is difficult. Cupfeeding with a correct technique - so that the infant controls intake, and milk is not "poured" into his mouth - was pioneered in Kenya by Musoke (1990), who found it easier to establish breastfeeding in preterm infants when bottles were no longer used.

9.3 Effect of artificial teats on breastfeeding

There are many reports from mothers and health professionals of difficulty getting infants who have bottle-fed to attach to the breast (Musoke, 1990; Mohrbacher & Stock, 1991; Riordan, 1991). Several differences, both mechanical and dynamic, have been described between suckling at the breast and suckling on an artificial teat (Ardran, 1958a and b; Woolridge, 1986a; Nowak, Smith & Erenberg, 1994). These suggest that using a teat may interfere with an infant learning to suckle. This is independent of the effect of the supplement on the infant's appetite. Some infants appear to develop a preference for an artificial teat, though the mechanism has not been fully explained (Neifert, Lawrence & Seacat, 1996). With sufficiently skilled care, individual infants can be helped to abandon the preference and suckle at the breast (Fisher & Inch, 1996), but such care is often not available and routine use of artificial teats may reduce overall breastfeeding rates.

Only two experimental studies have been identified and both have limitations. Cronenwett et al (1992) followed 121 infants. They were randomly assigned to a "total breastfeeding group" (who received $\leq$ 2 bottles per week from the second to the sixth week postpartum) and a "planned bottle group" (with one bottle of breastmilk or formula per day for at least 5 days per week during the same period). At 12 weeks postpartum 93% of the total breastfeeding group were still breastfeeding compared with 83% of the planned bottle group. At 6 months 69% and 59% were still breastfeeding, respectively. The trend shown may have become significant if the sample size had been larger. There was some suggestion of a dose response, with breastfeeding being more likely when fewer bottles were used.

Some 76% of infants were given bottles in hospital, regardless of group assignment. Multiple logistic regression analysis showed that 30% of all mothers whose infants were given bottles in hospital had severe breastfeeding problems, compared with only 14% of those whose infants were not given bottles (P=0.05).

Schubiger et al (1997), in a multicentre study in Switzerland, randomized 602 mothers and infants during their hospital stay either to an intervention group, who were intended to receive only medically indicated supplements, given by cup, with no artificial teats, or to a control group. At six months, no difference in the numbers breastfeeding was found between the two groups (57% versus 55%, respectively). Several major methodological limitations (see Table 9.1) reduce the internal validity of the study. For example, mothers were not in different rooms, making contamination likely; a large proportion in the intervention group (46%) did not comply, and only 8.3% of them did not receive supplements.

Jones (1994), in a small study in the United Kingdom, found that preterm infants who were cupfed when their mothers were not present to breastfeed them were more likely to continue to breastfeed than those who were given bottles.

Lang, Lawrence & Orme (1994) observed subsequent feeding patterns of 85 infants cupfed in hospital. The infants would otherwise have been bottle-fed, because of illness or prematurity. They were compared with 372 infants (365 mothers) who were not cupfed but their mother's intention was to breastfeed. Both groups had similar demographic, socioeconomic and postnatal characteristics. At discharge, 81% of the cupfed infants and 63% of the non-cupfed infants were exclusively breastfeeding, while 5% of the cupfed and 17% of the non-cupfed were only bottle-feeding. As the authors acknowledged, the nature of the study could not prove a cause and effect relationship, but suggest that giving cupfeeds may prevent the use of bottles, and help the establishment of breastfeeding.

9.4   Effect of pacifiers on breastfeeding

Pacifiers are generally used to calm an infant without giving a feed, and infants who use pacifiers may have fewer daily breastfeeds (Victora et al, 1997). When breast stimulation and milk removal are reduced, milk production decreases, which can lead to early termination of breastfeeding.

Righard & Alade (1997) reanalysed the results of a previous study of suckling technique (see Step 5) and pacifier use. Eighty-two fully breastfed term infants were enrolled and followed up by telephone 2 weeks, and 1, 2, 3 and 4 months after delivery. Most pacifier use (94%)

started before 2 weeks postpartum and before breastfeeding problems were reported. Breastfeeding problems were more common among mothers using pacifiers more than 2 h per day (83%) than among those using pacifiers occasionally or not at all (53%, P<0.05). Non-users were more likely to breastfeed at four months than users (91% versus 44%, P=0.03).

Pacifier users who were discharged with an incorrect suckling technique were less likely to be breastfeeding at four months than those discharged with a correct suckling technique (7% compared with 59%). Among non-users, there was no significant difference at four months between those with correct and incorrect suckling technique at discharge (90% and 82% respectively were still breastfeeding). Thus pacifier use appears to compound and increase a problem with suckling that might otherwise be overcome.

There have been three studies of pacifier use in Brazil (Victora et al, 1993; Barros et al, 1995a; Victora et al, 1997). Victora et al (1993) found that of 249 children still breastfeeding at one month of age, 72% of those using pacifiers 'full-time', and 59% using them 'part-time' had stopped breastfeeding by 6 months, compared with only 24% who did not use pacifiers at all (P<0.001). This suggests a possible dose response. Differences remained significant after controlling for confounders.

Barros et al (1995a) recruited 605 infants at birth in Brazil. At 1 month of age 23% were frequent users (using pacifiers during the whole day and at night) and 32% were part-time users. At 4 months, significantly more non-users were exclusively breastfeeding (45%) than frequent (17%) or partial users (26%)(P<0.001).

Pacifier users were nearly 4 times more likely to stop breastfeeding between 1 and 6 months of age than non users (relative risk 3.84, 95% CI 2.68-5.50; P<0.001). Even after adjusting for potential confounders such as perceived insufficiency of milk, the infant refusing the breast, and introduction of other feeds, the adjusted risk remained high (odds ratio 2.87, 95% CI 1.97-4.19) and significant (P<0.001).

In a combination of epidemiological and ethnographic studies, Victora et al (1997) visited 650 mothers and infants shortly after birth and at 1, 3 and 6 months, and a subsample (n=80) was visited 3 to 10 times (mean 4.5) to conduct in-depth interviews and direct observations. Almost half of the mothers took pacifiers to hospital and at 1 month 85% were using them, but changes in use patterns were common between 1 and 3 months. The 450 infants who were breastfed at 1 month and whose mothers did not report breastfeeding problems were analysed separately. The pattern of pacifier use at 1 month was strongly associated (P<0.001) with breastfeeding duration: non-users were 4 times more likely to continue breastfeeding at 6 months than full-time users. The crude risk of stopping breastfeeding between 1 and 6 months was high with the use of non-human milk (4.32, 95% CI 3.31-5.64) or full-time pacifier use (4.02, 95% CI 2.46-6.56) at 1 month. Using multivariate analysis, even after controlling for potential confounders (including maternal opinion on whether pacifiers affect breatfeeding) the risk remained high when using non-human milk (4.14, 3.09-5.54) or using a pacifier full-time (2.37, 1.40-4.01), and the effects were independent.

The ethnographic study showed that pacifier use is seen as a normal and desirable behaviour.

Mothers using pacifiers more intensely were also those who exercised a stronger control on their infant's breastfeeding behaviour, had stronger expectations about objective aspects of infant growth and development, and had anxious reactions to their infant's crying. Further analysis showed that they seemed more concerned with their social environment and more sensitive to social criticism, suggesting lack of self-confidence. The authors concluded that pacifiers may often be used as a mechanism to shorten and space breastfeeds, particularly by mothers with difficulty breastfeeding and a lack of confidence. Mothers who feel confident about breastfeeding seem to be less affected by pacifier use. Results also suggest that pacifiers can interfere with breastfeeding physiologically, but their use may be a marker of the desire to stop breastfeeding early rather than a cause of discontinuation. If so, then mothers may need additional support and counselling to help them to continue breastfeeding, and without this, educational campaigns aimed at reducing pacifier use are likely to fail.

9.5   Other effects of artificial teats and pacifiers

There are several short- and long-term outcomes associated with the use of artificial teats and pacifiers in infancy. Artificial teats alter infants' breathing and sucking patterns whether formula or expressed breastmilk is given (Mathew & Bhatia, 1989). Expiration is prolonged, and breathing frequency and oxygen saturation reduced with bottle-feeding, compared to breastfeeding.

Meier (1988) found that premature infants showed more signs of stress, such as lowered transcutaneous pO_2, when fed from a bottle than when suckling from the breast, suggesting that the practice of "teaching" a baby to bottle-feed before starting breastfeeding is inappropriate.

Changes in the oral cavity have also been reported. In older infants the rampant form of caries of the primary dentition, known as nursing caries, or 'baby bottle tooth decay', is most frequently seen with bottle-feeding or pacifier use (Milnes, 1996).

Dental malocclusion has been shown to be commoner in bottle-fed infants, the effect being greater with longer exposure. Labbok & Hendershot (1987) found in a retrospective cohort study of more than 9000 subjects that children 3 to 17 years old who were bottle-fed had 1.84 times higher risk of malocclusion than children who had been breastfed. Most comparative studies identified in a literature review (Drane, 1996) found an increased likelihood of malocclusion when artificial teats or pacifiers were used. These findings may be explained by a report by Inoue, Sakashita & Kamegai (1995), who found that masseter muscle activity, recorded by electromyography, was significantly less in bottle-fed than in breastfed 2-6 month-old infants. The masseter is the main muscle involved in mastication.

An increased incidence of acute and recurrent otitis media and its sequelae is seen with both bottle-feeding (Williamson, Dunleavey & Robinson, 1994) and pacifier use (Niemelä, Uhari & Möttönen, 1995). Abnormal tympanograms of infants aged 7-24 months bottle-fed in the supine position (Tully, Bar-Haim & Bradley, 1995) suggest an alteration of middle ear pressure dynamics. The authors suggest that the effect is due to Eustachian tube dysfunction, and reflux of fluid into the middle ear.

Other possible dangers include increased incidence of oral *Candida* infection (Manning, Coughlin & Poskitt, 1985; Sio et al, 1987); use of potentially carcinogenetic materials in manufacture of teats and pacifiers (Westin, 1990); and choking on separated pieces of rubber material.

9.6   Conclusions

There is growing evidence that the use of artificial teats and pacifiers is associated with early cessation of breastfeeding as well as some other problems. Several studies show the effects only of use after the perinatal period. However, the use of teats and pacifiers in maternities conveys the impression that health professionals consider them safe, making parents more likely to continue or start using them subsequently. Their use should be minimized, and avoided altogether if possible, to avoid giving families conflicting messages. Pacifiers should not be necessary at any time in maternity facilities.

The evidence for Step 9 needs to be considered with that for Step 6, concerning supplementary feeds. Supplements are often given by bottle, and it is difficult to separate the effect of the teat from that of the bottle contents, which may fill an infant's stomach and reduce the desire to breastfeed. However, the apparent advantages of cupfeeding suggest that the teat has an independent effect on breastfeeding.

Although difficulties in attaching a baby who has been bottle-fed to the breast may be overcome with sufficiently skilled help, such help is commonly not available. Infants should therefore not be unnecessarily exposed to the risk of needing it. Cups should be used in preference to bottles with teats for feeding infants who will later be breastfed, or when adequate sterilization is difficult.

Even if the use of pacifiers and feeding bottles is a marker of breastfeeding difficulties, as much as a cause of them, the conclusion is the same: health workers should be given more skill to enable them to provide appropriate help (see Step 2 and Step 6), both with the technique of breastfeeding, and to build mothers' confidence.

Table 9.1. RESULTS OF EXPERIMENTAL STUDY: USE OF FEEDING BOTTLES

Study [Methodology limitations]	Population characteristics	Control/Intervention	Sample size	Results		Conclusion
				Control	Intervention	
Cronenwett '92 (USA)	White, married primiparae who attended prenatal classes, intending to breastfeed, supported by breastfeeding consultant, followed up by telephone.	Control: mothers would, as much as possible, give one bottle of breast milk or formula per day for at least 5 days/week Int: mothers would give, as much as possible, not more than 2 bottles/week Both: bottles unrestricted up to 2 wks	Contr: 63 Int: 58 N = 121	9.4 bottles[a] given at week 6 52 (83%) still BF at 12 weeks	2 bottles[a] given at week 6 54 (93%) still BF at 12 weeks	Infants given 2 bottles less likely to stop BF at 12 weeks than infants given 9 bottles (not significant)
Schubiger '97 (Switzerland) [1, 2, 3]	Mothers intending to stay 5 days in hospital, planning to breastfeed ≥ 3 months, with healthy term infants. 10 hospitals with functioning BF programmes and policy of restricting formula use.	Control: bottles and pacifiers offered to all infants without restriction Int: dextrin-maltose solution (DM) given by cup or spoon if 'medically' indicated, artificial teats forbidden (Steps 6 + 9); 114 mothers did not fully comply due to use of pacifiers (70), use of bottles (19), failure to spoon/cupfeed (9) and other reasons (16).	Contr:291 Int: 180 N = 471	7.3 (0-24) DM feeds given during first 5 days* 55% still BF at 6 months 69-76% using pacifier at 2 and 4 months	6.1 (0-18) DM feeds given during first 5 days* 57% still BF at 6 months 69-76% using pacifier at 2 and 4 months	Using artificial teats in hospital did not increase likelihood of stopping BF at 6 months.

*P<0.05; **P<0.01; ***P<0.001.

[a]: Data obtained from figures

BF: breastfeeding

79

Table 9.2. LONGITUDINAL STUDY USING CUPS

Study	Population	Sample	Exposure	Results		Conclusion
				Exposed	Not exposed	
Lang '94 (England)	Term and preterm infants(<28 to 36 weeks) whose mothers intended to breastfeed but were in situations where BF was not possible	Exp: 76 Non-exp:372 N = 448	Use of cupfeeding (others bottle-fed)	62 (81%) exclusively BF at discharge	231 (63%) exclusively BF at discharge	Cupfeeding associated with increased likelihood of exclusive BF at discharge

BF: breastfeeding

Table 9.3. COMPARATIVE RESULTS OF LONGITUDINAL AND CROSS SECTIONAL STUDIES

USE OF PACIFIERS OR DUMMIES

Study	Population	Sample	Exposure	Results		Conclusion
				Exposed	Not exposed	
Victora '93 (Brazil)	All mothers with children under 2 years old living in 2 periurban poor areas; infants still BF at 1 month; full information available.	Exp: 119 Non-exp: 67 N = 186	Use of pacifiers at 1 month	77 (65%) stopped BF by 6 months*** Adjusted risk ratio: 3.0 (95% CI 1.9-4.6)	16 (24%) stopped BF by 6 months Adjusted risk ratio: 1.0	Pacifier use associated with increased risk of stopping BF by 6 months
Barros '95 (Brazil)	Rooming-in healthy newborns of urban low-income mothers, still BF at 1 month. 85.5% of initial sample (n = 605) followed-up for 6 months by home visits.	Exp I: 104 Exp II: 159 Non-exp: 242 N = 505	Use of pacifiers at 1 month: Exp I: Whole day and at night Exp II: Partial use	*Exclusive BF at 4 months:* Exp I: 18 (17%)*** Exp II: 42 (26%)*** Crude RR for stopping BF at 1-6 months: 3.84*** (95% CI 2.68-5.50). RR=2.87*** (Cox regr.)	*Exclusive BF at 4 months:* 108 (45%)*** RR=1.00***	Pacifier use associated with increased risk of stopping BF between 1 and 6 months
Victora '97 (Brazil)	Low-income mothers from a middle-sized city in southern Brazil, not reporting breastfeeding difficulties, still breastfeeding at 1 month	Exp I: 46 Exp II: 323 Non-exp: 81 N = 450	Use of pacifiers at 1 month: Exp I: Whole day and at night Exp II: Partial use	Exp I: 16% still BF at 6 months*** (OR for stopping BF by 6 months = 2.37, 95% CI 1.4-4.01) Exp II: 40% still BF at 6 months*** (OR = 1.74, 95% CI 1.15-2.63)	65% still BF at 6 months*** (OR = 1.00)	Pacifier use associated with higher risk of stopping BF at 3 and 6 months; more likely to affect less confident mothers
Righard '97 (Sweden)	Mothers fully breastfeeding healthy term infants. Follow-up by telephone for 4 months after delivery	Exp: 48 Non-exp: 34 N = 82	Extensive use of pacifiers: > 2 hours/day after discharge Limited use of pacifiers: < 2 h/day (n = 24)	20/24 (83%) of extensive users reported BF problems* 21/48 (44%) still BF at 4 months**: 59% if correct technique and 7% if incorrect*	31/58 (53%) of limited users and non-users reported BF problems* 31/34 (91%) still BF at 4 months**: 96% if correct technique and 82% if incorrect	Pacifier users more likely to stop BF before 4 months, likelihood increased if suckling technique not correct at discharge

*P<0.05; **P<0.01; ***P<0.001.   BF: breastfeeding   OR: Odds ratio

Proportion of infants who were breastfed up to 6 months of age according to frequency of pacifier use at 1 month

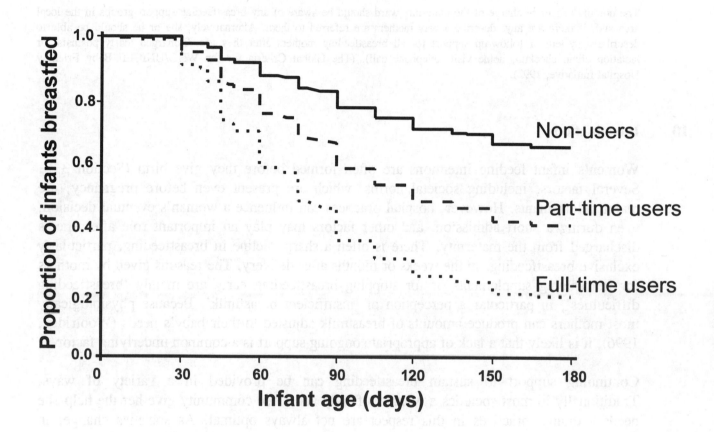

Non-users vs part-time users: P<0.001

Non-users vs full-time users: P<0.001

Source: Victora CG et al (1997) Pacifier use and short breastfeeding duration: cause, consequence or coincidence?
Reproduced by permission of *Pediatrics*, 99, pp. 445-453, copyright 1997.

STEP 10

10.1 **"Foster the establishment of breastfeeding support groups and refer mothers to them on discharge from the hospital or clinic."**

Mothers breastfeeding should be explored for their plans for infant feeding after discharge. They should also be able to describe one thing that has been recommended to ensure that they will be linked to a breastfeeding support group (if adequate support is not available in their own families) or report that the hospital will provide follow-up support on breastfeeding if needed.

The nursing officer in charge of the maternity ward should be aware of any breastfeeding support groups in the local area and, if there are any, describe a way mothers are referred to them. Alternatively, she or he should be able to describe a system of follow-up support for all breastfeeding mothers after they are discharged (early postnatal or lactation clinic checkup, home visit, telephone call). (The Global Criteria for the WHO/UNICEF Baby Friendly Hospital Initiative, 1992).

10.2 **Introduction**

Women's infant feeding intentions are often formed before they give birth (Section 3.3). Several factors, including societal norms, which are present even before pregnancy, are major determinants. However, hospital practices can influence a woman's eventual decision, even during a short admission, and other factors may play an important role after she is discharged from the maternity. There is often a sharp decline in breastfeeding, particularly exclusive breastfeeding, in the weeks or months after delivery. The reasons given by mothers for introducing supplements or for stopping breastfeeding early are mainly 'breastfeeding difficulties', in particular a perception of 'insufficient breastmilk'. Because physiologically most mothers can produce amounts of breastmilk adjusted to their baby's needs (Woolridge, 1996), it is likely that a lack of appropriate ongoing support is a common underlying factor.

Continuing support to sustain breastfeeding can be provided in a variety of ways. Traditionally in most societies a woman's family and close community give her the help she needs - though practices in this respect are not always optimal. As societies change, in particular with urbanization, support from health workers, or from friends who are also mothers and from the child's father, becomes more important. Perez-Escamilla et al (1993) in a study of 165 low-income urban Mexican women, found that full breastfeeding up to 4 months postpartum was consistently associated with support and approval from the male partner or the mother's mother. Bryant (1982) suggests that "geographical proximity of network members has a significant effect on the role of relatives, friends and neighbors in infant feeding patterns. The relative importance of health care professionals as information sources is influenced by the location and accessibility of network members."

In some countries, for example in Scandinavia, mother-to-mother support groups have been major players in breastfeeding promotion. In other countries, such groups hardly exist and may not be appropriate. This step is thus interpreted to include all forms of ongoing support that may be available or that can be developed.

In both industrialized and developing countries health professionals have difficulty in providing adequate follow-up care and mothers may be reluctant to seek help from the formal health service if difficulties with breastfeeding arise. There is thus a need to involve the community in providing appropriate support.

10.3 Effect of post-discharge support on breastfeeding: Health services

Thirteen randomized or comparative controlled studies were identified which measured the effect on breastfeeding of early support after discharge (with or without other interventions) through health services. Eight of the studies reported significant differences in outcomes, measured between 4 weeks and 6 months after birth (Houston et al, 1981; Saner et al, 1985; Jones & West, 1986; Frank et al, 1987; Jenner, 1988; Saunders & Carroll, 1988; Neyzi et al, 1991a and 1991b), 1 reported borderline significance (Bloom et al, 1982b, P=0.05), and 4 reported no effect (Hall, 1978; Grossman, Harter & Kay, 1987; Grossman et al, 1990; Chung-Hey, 1993).

Houston et al (1981) studied postnatal support in Scotland. The control group received an average of 2.7 routine home visits by health visitors. The intervention group received in addition a visit in the postnatal ward and an average of 11.5 home visits over 24 weeks, as well as being given a telephone contact number in case of difficulties. The intervention group were significantly more likely to be breastfeeding at 12 and 20 weeks.

Jones & West (1986), in Wales, assigned mothers attempting to breastfeed to an intervention (n=228) or a control group (n=355). The intervention group were visited by a lactation nurse in hospital and at home an unspecified number of times. Any breastfeeding at 4 weeks was more prevalent in the intervention group (P<0.005), particularly in lower socioeconomic groups.

Frank et al (1987) in the United States assessed 2 interventions, postnatal support and non-commercial discharge packs (see step 6). Two groups received one 20- to 40-minute session with a breastfeeding counsellor in hospital and 8 telephone calls. Two other groups received routine postpartum nursing contacts and a discharge teaching session with some breastfeeding content. Full breastfeeding at 2 months and any breastfeeding at 3 months were significantly more likely in the groups receiving extra counselling.

In Bangladesh, a randomized controlled study of infants aged up to 12 weeks measured the effect of breastfeeding counselling in a diarrhoeal disease hospital (Haider et al, 1996). Counsellors were trained using the WHO/UNICEF 40-hour *Breastfeeding Counselling: A training course* (WHO, 1993). The mothers of 250 partially breastfed infants admitted for treatment of diarrhoea were randomly allocated to receive either three individual counselling sessions, two in hospital and one at home one week later (intervention group); or routine group health education in hospital (controls). Two weeks later 75% of infants in the intervention group were exclusively breastfeeding compared with only 8% in the control group (P<0.001).

A cohort study in Brazil focused on breastfeeding counselling in health facilities. Barros et al (1995b) followed 605 low- to middle-income Brazilian mothers and infants to 6 months of age. Infants who attended lactation centres (73% attended three times or more) were more likely to be breastfeeding exclusively than non-attenders at 4 months (43% versus 18% respectively) and at 6 months (15% versus 6%). Attenders also had fewer episodes of illness, and better weight gain than non-attenders.

10.4 Effect of post-discharge support on breastfeeding: Mother-to-mother support groups

Few studies of mother-to-mother support groups have been published. One cross-sectional study (Meara, 1976) conducted in the USA found that mothers affiliated to La Leche League (LLL) were more likely than non-affiliated mothers to breastfeed on demand in hospital (60% versus 29% respectively) and to delay the introduction of solid foods until 4 to 6 months (87% versus 31% respectively). However, the effect of mother-to-mother support cannot be evaluated because of the inevitable self-selection.

A study in Guatemala (Maza et al, unpublished document, 1997) showed that the activities of LLL of Guatemala's mother-to-mother breastfeeding promotion and support project in periurban areas were sustained even after funding ended. Breastfeeding counsellors provided individual and group support, and appeared to be effective for helping individual mothers. However, as acknowledged by the authors, only 30% of the target population (pregnant women, mothers of children under 24 months and other women of childbearing age) knew of the existence of breastfeeding support groups, and only 37% of those had ever attended a group.

10.5 Effect of post-discharge support on breastfeeding: Community-based peer counsellors

To date, nine studies have assessed the effect on breastfeeding of support by peer counsellors or health promoters, sometimes in conjunction with health professionals (Burkhalter & Marin, 1991; R Lundgren et al, unpublished document, 1992; Kistin, Abramson & Dublin, 1994; Mongeon & Allard, 1995; Long et al, 1995; Alvarado et al, 1996; Davies-Adetugbo, 1996; AL Morrow et al, unpublished document, 1996; Leite et al, 1998). All studies except one (Mongeon & Allard, 1995) reported an increase in exclusive or partial breastfeeding, measured up to 6 months after birth.

Burkhalter & Marin (1991) studied 3 groups of suburban Chilean mothers of mixed socioeconomic status, 1 group before and 2 groups after the intervention. The intervention groups received both prenatal and postnatal support, but the authors considered the postnatal support the most important. It consisted of monthly follow-up in the well-baby clinic with specific protocols for mothers intending to start bottle-feeding, 8 home visits from a program staff member, peer group encouragement and additional weekly visits when difficulties arose. At 6 months the intervention groups had significantly higher full breastfeeding rates (P<0.001).

Davies-Adetugbo (1996) assessed a community-based health education programme in Nigeria which included mothers' exposure to breastfeeding posters and handouts, talks at clinics and at home, and one-to-one counselling by trained community health workers. Full breastfeeding at 4 months was significantly more frequent in the intervention group (40%, 30%-50%) than among controls (14%, 8%-21%).

A study from Mexico (AL Morrow et al, unpublished document, 1996) reported that mothers receiving 6 home visits by trained lay counsellors (*promotoras*) were significantly more likely to be exclusively breastfeeding at 3 months (72%) than those receiving 3 home visits by the same counsellors (50%, P<0.001). Both groups were significantly more likely to be exclusively breastfeeding at 3 months than a concurrent control group (7%, P<0.001).

In a brief communication, Fukumoto & Creed (1994) reported that a community-based programme in Peru, which included prenatal and postnatal education, increased the number of exclusively breastfed infants 2 to 4 months old. The effect of education was due to a decrease in the use of herbal teas and waters, but there was no change in the number of women using other milks, suggesting that mother's confidence in their breastmilk was insufficiently raised by the intervention.

Preliminary results from a controlled study in Fortaleza, Brazil (Leite et al, 1998), indicate that community counsellors can increase predominant breastfeeding rates at 1 month. Mothers and their infants, whose mean birth weight was 2,690g (range 1,770-2,900g), were randomly assigned to an intervention group (n=385) visited by community counsellors three times during the first month postpartum (intervention group) or a control group (n=455). At one month postpartum, mothers in the intervention group were more likely to be breastfeeding predominantly (65%) than the controls (51%).

10.6   Conclusions

A number of different kinds of postnatal breastfeeding support seem to be effective in sustaining breastfeeding up to 3-4 months, and in one group up to 6 months. It is probably an advantage if support starts before discharge from the maternity facility, to enable mothers to establish breastfeeding, and to prevent difficulties. A combination of antenatal, in-hospital, and post-discharge support are likely to act synergistically. A mother's immediate family, especially her male partner and her baby's grandmothers, and close friends, should be involved, as they may have an important influence on breastfeeding practices.

It is not possible to say how many hours of support are necessary to achieve a particular result, though studies do seem to suggest that more frequent contacts may have more effect.

It is also not clear exactly what kind of intervention is most effective. One-to-one counselling and help targeted at specific difficulties or crises of the mothers' confidence may be the most useful. Telephone calls appear not to be useful on their own.

There is an urgent need to explore the potential of community groups and counsellors further. They may be more able than formal health services to provide the frequent one-to-one help that mothers need to build their confidence and to overcome difficulties. Possibly a combination of day-to-day support from the community backed up by more specialised help from health services when the need arises could be more effective than either alone.

Comparison of the percent of mothers exclusively breastfeeding their infants during the past week in intervention groups (3-visit and 6-visit) and control groups

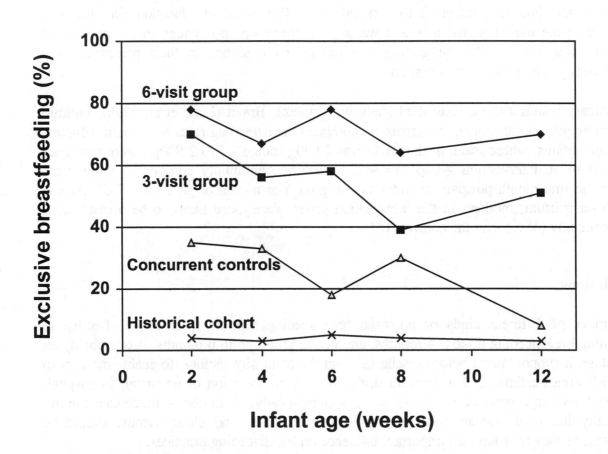

3-visit and 6-visit intervention groups vs concurrent controls: P<0.001

6-visit group vs 3-visit group: P<0.001

Concurrent control vs historical cohort: P<0.001

Source: Morrow et al (1996) The effectiveness of home-based counseling to promote exclusive breastfeeding among Mexican mothers. In: *Exclusive breastfeeding promotion: a summary of findings from EPB`s applied research program (1992-1996).* Wellstart International`s Expanded Promotion of Breastfeeding (EPB) Program (unpublished document).

Table 10.1. COMPARATIVE RESULTS OF EXPERIMENTAL STUDIES CONTINUING SUPPORT – HEALTH SERVICES

Study [Methodology limitations]	Population characteristics	Control/Intervention	Sample Size	Results Control	Results Intervention	Conclusion
Hall '78 (USA)	Married, middle-class, first-time BF mothers	Control I: routine hospital care Control II: as above + slide-tape presentation + pamphlet. Int: as control II + in-hospital visits + 2 phone calls + counsellor available by telephone if needed	Contr I: 12 Contr II: 13 Int: 15 N = 40	6 (50%) still BF at 6 weeks in Contr I, 6 (50%) still BF at 6 weeks in Contr II	12 (80%) still BF at 6 weeks	Non significant increase in any BF at 6 weeks
Houston '81 (Scotland)	Urban breastfeeding mothers with healthy term infants	Control: routine care from community services Int: hospital visit + 11 home visits + counsellor available by telephone if needed	Contr: 52 Int: 28 N = 80	40 (78%) still BF at 12 weeks 33 (64%) still BF at 20 weeks	28 (100%) still BF at 12 weeks** 25 (88%) still BF at 20 weeks*	Home support beneficial (any BF) at 20 weeks
Bloom '82 (Canada) [8]	Married primiparae with healthy infants, Apgar 5 at 5 min, vaginal deliveries	Control: pamphlet about BF techniques Int: as control + 3 weekly telephone calls for 5-10 min from day 10 offering advice + referral if requested	Contr: 49 Int: 50 N = 99	Mean duration of BF: 21.0 days	Mean duration of BF: 28.6 days	BF duration increased one week (P = 0.05)
Saner '85 (Turkey) [5, 8]	Low income healthy mothers with healthy term infants, with little information about infant nutrition	Control: contact at 1 month Int I: 3 in-hospital sessions on advantages of BF + monthly visits Int II: 1 in-hospital session on advantages of BF + 1 visit at 3 months postpartum	Contr: 35 Int I: 40 Int II: 14 N = 89	20% were fully BF at 3 months***	Int I: 95% were fully BF at 3 months*** Int II: 50% were fully BF at 3 months***	Full BF increased with postpartum information on advantages of BF
Jones '86 (Wales)	Primiparae and multiparae attempting to breastfeed	Control: routine hospital care Int: visits by lactation nurse in hospital and at home to provide counselling	Contr: 355 Int: 228 N = 583	256 (72%) still BF at 4 weeks** 99 (28%)[a] still BF at 6 months**	192 (84%) still BF at 4 weeks** 87 (38%)[a] still BF at 6 months**	Home visits beneficial (any BF) at 6 months
Frank '87 (USA)	Urban predominantly low-income non-white BF mothers, healthy newborns	Control: routine support + commercial pack Int I: research support (in-hospital + 8 phone calls + 24-hour telephone paging service) + BF pack Int II: research support + commercial pack Int III: routine support + BF pack	Contr: 83 Int I: 79 Int II: 84 Int III: 78 N = 324	Fully BF at 2 months: 17 (20%)	Fully BF at 2 months: 34 (43%) in Int I**, 24 (29%) in Int II, 22 (28%) in Int III	Extra support beneficial (full BF) when BF discharge pack added

*P < 0.05; **P < 0.01; ***P < 0.001.

BF: breastfeeding

[a] : Data recalculated

Table 10.1. (Cont.) COMPARATIVE RESULTS OF EXPERIMENTAL STUDIES CONTINUING SUPPORT – HEALTH SERVICES

Study [Methodology limitations]	Population characteristics	Control/Intervention	Sample Size	Results Control	Results Intervention	Conclusion
Grossman '87 (USA) [1, 2, 5]	Low-income women who received prenatal care, intending to breastfeed	Control: routine in-hospital assistance with BF Int: intensive in-hospital counselling + telephone contact on days 2, 4, 7-10 and 3 and 6 weeks for support and counselling + "24-hour helpline".	N = 76 Groups not specified	77% still BF at 6 weeks	73% still BF at 6 weeks	Postpartum support via telephone only not beneficial
Jenner '88 (England)	White working class married primiparae intending to BF	Control: 1 antenatal structured home interview + brief hospital visit Int: as above + 2 antenatal home visits + 2-3 home visits + telephone contact available	Contr: 19 Int: 19 N = 38	4 (21%) fully BF at 3 months	13 (68%) fully BF at 3 months**	Prenatal and postnatal visits increased full BF
Saunders '88 (USA) [1, 6]	Rural low-income predominantly Hispanic women enrolled in food program	Control (pre-int): routine care Int I: 1 hospital visit + 1 phone call at 4-5 days postpartum + 1 support class at 2 wk Int II: 1 or 2 of above interventions	Contr: 75 Int I: 36 Int II: 44 N = 155	Still BF at 16 weeks: 35 (47%)	Still BF at 16 weeks: 24 (67%) in Int I*, 16 (37%) [a] in Int II	Combined postpartum support increased any BF at 16 weeks
Grossman '90 (USA) [4]	Low income women with full term healthy newborns, intending BF at birth	Control: routine teaching before discharge, by obstetrical nursing staff Int: 1 hospital visit + phone calls at 2, 4 and 7-10 days + 3 weeks postpartum	Contr: 48 Int: 49 N = 97	Median duration of any BF: 14.8 weeks 10/44 (23%) still BF at 6 months	Median duration of any BF: 8 weeks 7/49 (14%%) still BF at 6 months	Telephone calls not beneficial (any BF)
Neyzi '91a (Turkey) [4]	Urban primaparae with vaginal deliveries, healthy newborns >2500 g birthweight, from a social security hospital	Control: home visit on day 5-7 (hygiene and general baby care) Int: hospital session included 1 film on BF and 40-minute education on BF practice; 20-30 minute home visit on day 5-7 + booklet Both: 1 hospital group session with film on diarrhoeal disease; monthly follow-up	Contr: 442 Int: 499 N = 941	12% exclusively BF at 1 week***, 2% at 2 months*	47% exclusively BF at 1 week***, 4.3% at 2 months*	Exclusive BF at 1 week more likely if support (film, home visit) provided
Neyzi '91b (Turkey) [4]	Same as above	Control: same as above Int: same as above + follow up by paediatric resident at 2 wk, and 1, 2, 3 and 4 months (with close relative)	Contr: 442 Int: 96 N = 538	61% fully BF at 1 month***, 5% at 4 months***	85% fully BF at 1 month***, 68% at 4 months***	Continued support increased full BF at 4 months

*P<0.05; **P<0.01; ***P<0.001.   [a] : Data recalculated

BF: breastfeeding

88

Table 10.1. (Cont.) COMPARATIVE RESULTS OF EXPERIMENTAL STUDIES

CONTINUING SUPPORT – HEALTH SERVICES

Study [Methodology limitations]	Population characteristics	Control/Intervention	Sample Size	Results		Conclusion
				Control	Intervention	
Chung-Hey '93 (Taiwan, China)	Mothers of term healthy newborns, BF at discharge, able to read Chinese	Control: no intervention Int I: home visits by nurse at weeks 1, 2, 4 and 8 after discharge Int II: telephone calls by nurse at weeks 1, 2, 4 and 8 after discharge	Contr: 60 Int I: 60 Int II: 60 N = 180	Mean duration of BF: Contr: 3.35 weeks Reason for stopping BF was insufficient milk in 40%	Mean duration of BF: Int I: 4.1 weeks Int II: 3.6 weeks Reason for stopping was insufficient milk in 43% (Int I) and 38% (Int II)	Home visits or telephone calls did not affect BF duration
Haider '96 (Bangladesh)	Infants ≤12 weeks of age, with diarrhoea of less than 5 days' duration, weight-for-age >60% of NCHS median, still breastfeeding.	Control: routine BF advice during hospital stay Int: 3 BF counselling sessions during hospital stay for diarrhoea management + 1 session at home 1 week after discharge	Contr: 125 Int: 125 N = 250	7 (6%) exclusively BF at discharge*** 8/103 (8%)*** exclusively BF 2 weeks after discharge	74 (60%) exclusively BF at discharge*** 78/104 (75%)*** exclusively BF 2 weeks after discharge	Counselling beneficial (EBF) 2 weeks after discharge

*P<0.05; **P<0.01; ***P<0.001.   BF: breastfeeding

89

Table 10.2. COMPARATIVE RESULTS OF EXPERIMENTAL STUDIES
CONTINUING SUPPORT – COMMUNITY-BASED COUNSELLORS

Study [Methodology limitations]	Population characteristics	Control/Intervention	Sample Size	Results Control	Results Intervention	Conclusion
Burkhalter '91 (Chile) [1, 6]	All births registered in a suburban health centre area with mixed socioeconomic status	Control (pre-int): prenatal routine care, well baby clinic Group I: 4 prenatal lectures + monthly controls + 8 home visits in 6 mo + peer group encouragement. Group II: As above, 1 year after changes introduced.	Contr: 137 Int I: 115 Int II: 117 N = 369	46 (34%) fully BF at 6 months	Int I: 74 (64%) fully BF at 6 months*** Int II: 64 (55%) fully BF at 6 months***	Prenatal and postnatal support beneficial (full BF) at 6 months
Lundgren, '92 (Honduras) [1]	Rural villages with limited access to water, latrines and health services	Control: BF promotion activities (monthly meetings, distribution of educational materials) led by Rural Health Committees in 20 villages Int: same BF promotion activities, led by village-based volunteers trained on BF counselling, in 20 villages Group targeted (both): pregnant women and mothers of infants <1 year old	Contr(pre): 209 Contr(post): 226 Int (pre): 207 Int (post): 221 N = 863	Median duration of exclusive BF (pre/post-survey): 1.3/1.2 months Exclusive BF at 2 months (pre/post): 20%/18%**(C vs Int)	Median duration of exclusive BF (pre/post-survey): 1.2/3 months Exclusive BF at 2 months (pre/post): 20%/50%***	Exclusive BF increased in villages where support by trained BF workers existed
Kistin '94 (USA)	Low-income urban women intending to breastfeed, who requested peer support	Control: no counsellor Int: peer counsellor telephone calls (≥2/week until BF established, then every 1-2 weeks)	Contr: 43 Int: 59 N = 102	Mean duration of any BF: 8 weeks* Mean duration of full BF: 4 wks*	Mean duration of any BF: 15 weeks* Mean duration of full BF: 8 wks*	Peer counsellor supported mothers breastfeed longer
Mongeon '95 (Canada) [7]	Pregnant women without previous experience breastfeeding, intending to breastfeed	Control: no additional support Int: 1 home visit (pre-birth) + weekly (6 wks) and bi-weekly telephone follow up by volunteer Both: 1 home visit by community nurse, other contacts initiated by mother	Contr: 100 Int: 100 N = 200	Insufficient milk: 45% (other data unclear)	Insufficient milk: 37%	Support by volunteer not beneficial
Long et al '95 (USA) [4]	Native American low-income pregnant women	Control (pre-int): prenatal routine care Int: prenatal and postnatal (at 1, 2 and 4-6 weeks postpartum) contact with peer counsellor by telephone, home visits and/or clinic visits	Contr: 67 Int: 41 N = 108	Among women followed up 3 months, 70% started BF; 36% were still BF at 3 months	Among women followed up 3 months, 84% started BF (P=0.05); 49% were still BF at 3 months	Peer counsellor support beneficial (any BF) at 3 months

*P<0.05; **P<0.01; ***P<0.001.

BF: breastfeeding

90

Table 10.2. (Cont.) COMPARATIVE RESULTS OF EXPERIMENTAL STUDIES CONTINUING SUPPORT – COMMUNITY-BASED COUNSELLORS

Study [Methodology limitations]	Population Characteristics	Control/Intervention	Sample Size	Results		Conclusion
				Control	Intervention	
Alvarado '96 (Chile) [1, 6, 8]	Low income mothers living in unsatisfactory sanitary conditions, in a periurban area.	Control: management of acute illnesses by physician and monitoring (1, 2, 4 and 6 months) by nurse at health centre. Int: home visits by community-based health promoters, group education (pre-birth and monthly thereafter) + 8 contacts with physician and midwife at health centre, until 6 months postpartum	Contr: 66 Int: 62 N = 128	8% fully BF at 4 months** 0% fully BF at 6 months**	90% fully BF at 4 months** 42% fully BF at 6 months**	Full BF more likely up to 6 months with support by health promoters
Davies-Adetugbo '96 (Nigeria) [6]	Late trimester pregnant women from 6 predominantly Yoruba farming communities	Control: routine care in antenatal clinics in PHC facilities, home visits (BF problems referred). Drop-outs: 21 (lost, stillbirths or infant deaths) Int: ≥3 counselling sessions before delivery + postpartum monthly home visits (message reinforcement, most BF problems solved). Drop-outs: 28 (lost, stillbirths or infant deaths)	Contr: 130 Int: 126 N = 256	6/108 (6%) started suckling within 30 min after birth 15/108 (14%) fully BF at 4 months	31/98 (32%) started suckling within 30 min after birth 39/98 (40%) fully BF at 4 months	Prenatal and postnatal support beneficial (full BF) at 4 months
Morrow, '96 (Mexico)	Predominantly low-income pregnant women in a periurban area of Mexico City	Concurrent control (CC): routine care in clinic Historical cohort (HC): pre-intervention Int I: 1 home visit at end of pregnancy + 1 visit soon after birth + 1 visit at end of week 2, by promotoras trained by LLL (Mexico) Int II: 2 home visits during pregnancy + 4 home postpartum visits soon after birth, and at 2, 4 and 8 weeks, by same promotoras	[HC: 316] CC: 15 Int I: 40 Int II: 25 N = 80	35% of CC exclusively BF at 2 weeks, and 7% at 12 weeks***(CC vs HC, CC vs both Int) Only 3-6% of HC exclusively BF in the week prior to interview***	70% of Int I exclusively BF at 2 weeks, and 50% at 12 weeks*** (Int I vs Int II) 79% of Int II exclusively BF at 2 weeks, and 72% at 12 weeks***	Home visits by trained promotoras had a beneficial dose-response effect on exclusive BF for at least first 3 months
Leite '98 (Brazil)	Mothers with healthy newborns weighing <3,000g born in 8 maternities	Control: routine care in health services Int: 3 home visits (days 5, 15 and 30 after birth) by lay counsellors	Contr: 455 Int: 385 N = 840	51% predominantly BF at 1 month	65% predominantly BF at 1 month (RR=0.56, 95% CI 0.42-0.75)	3 visits by lay counsellors improved predominant BF at 1 month

*P<0.05; **P<0.01; ***P<0.001.

BF: breastfeeding

Table 10.3. COMPARATIVE RESULTS OF LONGITUDINAL AND CROSS SECTIONAL STUDIES

CONTINUING SUPPORT

Study	Population Characteristics	Sample size	Exposure	Results		Conclusion
				Not exposed	Exposed	
Meara '76 (USA) [9]	La Leche League members: mainly highly educated middle income housewives whose BF experience occurred only before (not exposed) or only after affiliation (exposed).	Exp: 436 Non-exp: 117 N = Not clearly specified	Affiliation to La Leche League prior to BF experience. Not exposed group: usually pregnant women attending meetings to prepare for an additional BF experience.	34/117 (29%) demand fed in hospital 13/42 (31%) started solids at 4-6 months	262/436 (60%) demand fed in hospital 379/436 (87%) started solids at 4-6 months	Affiliation to La Leche League associated with increased knowledge, attitudes and practices
Barros '95 (Brazil)	Rooming-in healthy newborns of low to middle income urban mothers. Follow-up for 6 months.	Exp: 289 Non-exp: 246 N = 535	Attendance at lactation centre	44 (18%) exclusively BF at 4 months At 6 months, 15 (6%) exclusively BF, 135 (55%) still BF****	124 (43%) exclusively BF at 4 months*** At 6 months, 43 (15%) exclusively BF, 197 (68%) still BF***	Attendance at lactation centres significantly associated with exclusive BF at 4 months

*P<0.05; **P<0.01; ***P<0.001.   BF: breastfeeding

COMBINED INTERVENTIONS

11.1   Introduction

The preceding sections have reviewed evidence for the 'Ten Steps', considering each Step as far as possible as an isolated intervention. However, as is already apparent, a number of studies included several steps together, and appear to show that combined interventions can have more effect on breastfeeding than any step singly. For all practical purposes, this must be considered one of the most important conclusions of this review.

11.2   Effect on breastfeeding practices

Seven studies were identified in which the effect of more than one breastfeeding promotion intervention could be differentiated. Six of them showed a significant increase in breastfeeding (Frank et al, 1987; Saunders & Carroll, 1988; Strachan-Lindenberg, Cabrera & Jimenez, 1990; Altobelli et al, 1991; Perez-Escamilla et al, 1992; Pugin et al, 1996).

An early study by Salariya, Easton & Cater (1978) in the UK found that mothers who both initiated breastfeeding within 10 minutes and then continued giving 2-hourly feeds were more likely to breastfeed at 12 weeks than mothers who started later and breastfed 4-hourly. However, the numbers were small and the results did not reach significance.

Frank et al in the USA (1987) found that women who received both a breastfeeding promotion package at discharge and additional breastfeeding counselling, both in-hospital and after discharge, were the more likely to be breastfeeding at 1 month, than women who received only one of these interventions. Saunders & Carroll (1988) found that three simple interventions combined (one in-hospital guidance session, one telephone call and one post-discharge breastfeeding class) had a significant effect on breastfeeding, but none of the interventions had any effect alone.

Perez-Escamilla et al (1992) in Mexico found an increase in full breastfeeding at 4 months when rooming-in and breastfeeding guidance were combined, while the effect of rooming-in alone lasted for only one month. Similarly, Strachan-Lindenberg, Cabrera & Jimenez (1990) found that when breastfeeding guidance was combined with rooming-in there was an increase in breastfeeding at both 1 week and at 4 months, but when breastfeeding guidance was combined with early contact, the effect was only significant at 1 week.

Pugin et al in Chile (1996) compared a pre-intervention control group of women with a group exposed to a breastfeeding promotion programme which included five interventions (Valdes et al, 1993): training of the health team, activities at the prenatal clinic and in the hospital (earlier initial contact, breastfeeding guidance, reduction of supplements, reinforcement of rooming-in), creation of an outpatient lactation clinic and offering the Lactational Amenorrhea Method (LAM) as an initial form of family planning. At 6 months postpartum full breastfeeding was significantly higher in the intervention group (67%) than in the control group (32%, P<0.0001), even after controlling for parity. A subgroup receiving additional antenatal education was more likely to breastfeed fully (80%) than the subgroup with the same interventions but without additional education (65%, P<0.005) (discussed with Step 3).

Another 10 comparative studies were identified which looked at the effect of various combinations of breastfeeding promotion interventions together. From these studies some common patterns emerge: breastfeeding support or counselling after discharge, when combined with in-hospital or antenatal counselling, is particularly likely to increase breastfeeding. Some authors considered that postnatal support, through peer groups, home visits or clinic follow-up, was the most important component (Burkhalter & Marin, 1991).

Negative interactions are also possible when harmful practices such as the use of formula continue. Reiff & Essock-Vitale (1985) studied the feeding practices of 77 mothers who delivered in a hospital where educational materials, counselling, support and policies were generally favourable to breastfeeding but formula was still used. Nursing staff's attitudes regarding breastfeeding were positive: more than 80% reported discussing the advantages of breastfeeding routinely with mothers. However, 59 (77%) mothers had started bottle-feeding 2 to 3 weeks after delivery, the majority (93%) remembered which brand had been used in hospital and 52 (88%) were using that brand. Parents may interpret the routine use of formula in nurseries as an endorsement by health staff, in spite of clear verbal messages promoting breastfeeding.

Thus a few interventions, under experimental conditions, can improve breastfeeding attitudes or practices to some extent (Houston et al, 1981; Jones & West, 1986; Jenner, 1988; Long et al, 1995; Davies-Adetugbo, 1996). However, when interventions are part of a well-established programme, they appear to be more effective (Hardy et al, 1982; Popkin et al, 1991; Nylander et al, 1991; Burkhalter & Marin, 1991, Lutter et al, 1997). Benefits are most likely to be realized when interventions are strengthened by institutional policy and potentially harmful practices are discontinued. In Brazil, Lutter et al (1997) compared a hospital with an active breastfeeding promotion programme with a nearby control hospital where rooming-in was in place and formula was restricted, but with a lower level of coverage of information and support activities. Women in the programme hospital were more likely to receive information and support, and the median duration of exclusive breastfeeding was 75 days - 53 days longer than in the control hospital.

11.3   Effect of combined interventions on cost-effectiveness and morbidity

Breastfeeding promotion programmes implemented through maternity services can be one of the most cost-effective health interventions for gaining disability-adjusted life years (DALYs), preventing cases of diarrhoea, and preventing deaths from diarrhoea (Horton et al, 1996). Programmes implemented in Brazil, Honduras and Mexico were assessed, and it was found that cost-effectiveness was highest when programmes included the removal of formula and reduced the use of medications during delivery. This is partly because the cost of these interventions are minimal and may even result in savings. Investment in hospital-based education and mothers' support was still extremely cost-effective, though less than removal of

94

formula, because education requires more time and skill and is therefore intrinsically more costly. Support, education and counselling for mothers are introduced more slowly than other interventions and additional effort is required for their implementation. While removal of formula and rooming-in may be essential prerequisites in breastfeeding initiation, the activities related to direct support and information have the greatest impact in extending the duration of exclusive breastfeeding (Lutter et al 1997).

95

Proportion of exclusive breastfeeding (EBF): survival curves by Hospital, Santos, Brazil, 1992-93

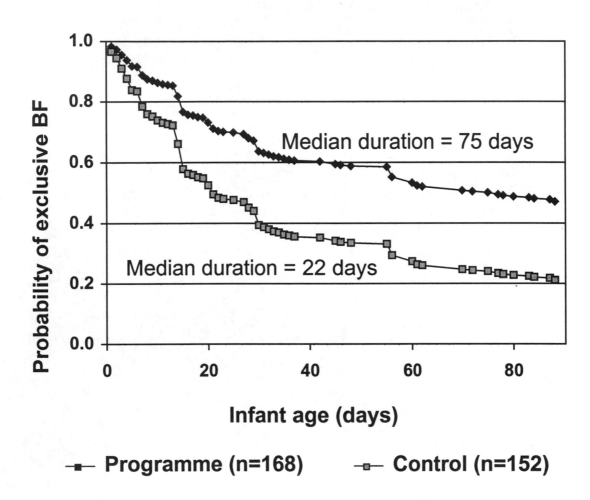

Median duration = 75 days

Median duration = 22 days

Programme (n=168)   Control (n=152)

Programme hospital vs Control hospital: P<0.0001

Table 11.1. COMPARATIVE RESULTS OF EXPERIMENTAL STUDIES COMBINED INTERVENTIONS - DIFFERENTIATED EFFECTS

Study [Methodology limitations]	Control	Intervention[a]	General Results	Table
Salariya '78 (Scotland) [8]	Late contact, nursing every 4 hours	I: 4 + partial 8 (early contact, 2-hour nursing). II: 4 (early contact). III: partial 8 (2-hour nursing).	Increase (not statistically significant) of any BF with early contact and 2-hour feedings combined.	4.1 8.1
Frank '87 (USA)	Routine advice + commercial discharge pack	I: 5+10 (BF counselling) + commercial discharge pack. II: 5+10+BF discharge pack. III: routine advice + BF discharge pack.	Significant effect (full BF) of combined interventions at 1 month. Significant effect of each intervention independently.	6.4 10.1
Saunders '88 (USA) [1, 6]	Interventions omitted	5+10: BF guidance in hospital, one contact at 4-5 days and/or one structured class at 2 weeks.	BF duration increased significantly up to 16 weeks only when 3 activities were combined.	10.1
Strachan-Lindenberg '90 (Nicaragua) [8]	Complete mother-infant separation until discharge	I: 4+5 (early contact and standardized BF messages). II: 5 (standardized BF messages) +7.	Significant effect (full BF) at 1 week with either intervention group. Effect (any BF) at 4 months significant only if rooming-in with BF guidance.	4.1 5.1 7.1
Altobelli '91 (Peru)	Partial rooming-in	Hosp A and B: 2+5 (training + development of standardized BF messages). Partial steps 6-9 already established in both.	Significant increase of EBF at 4 weeks in hospitals with training. Significant longer term effect (12 weeks) in hosp A (extensive exposure to BF messages) vs hosp B (moderate exposure).	2.1 5.1
Perez-Escamilla '92 (Mexico)	Some formula discharge samples given	I: 7 (rooming-in). II: 5+7 (BF guidance [standard messages] and rooming-in). No formula samples given in both.	Long-term significant effect (full BF) of rooming-in with BF guidance among primiparae, but only short-term effect if rooming-in only. No effect on multiparae.	5.1 7.1
Pugin '96 (Chile) [6]	Pre-int: partial rooming-in	I: 1-3 and 5-10 (+ earlier initial contact). II: as above + intensive Step 3.	A significant increase in full BF at 6 months was shown with 9 steps. Adding intensive antenatal education resulted in a further significant increase.	3.1

[a]: Numbers refer to Steps 1-10   BF: breastfeeding

Table 11.2. COMPARATIVE RESULTS OF EXPERIMENTAL STUDIES

COMBINED INTERVENTIONS - GROUPED

Study [Methodology limitations]	Control	Intervention[a]	General Results	Table
Houston '81 (Scotland)	Routine visit by community health staff	5 + 10: BF counselling in hospital and after discharge.	Significant increase in BF rate at 12 and 20 weeks in intervention group.	10.1
Hardy '82 (Brazil) [6]	Interventions omitted, no rooming-in	2 + 5 + 10: training, BF counselling in hospital and after discharge). Rooming-in already practiced.	Significant increase in full and any BF in intervention group up to 9 months. No changes among women <25 years, those with less education or with partners <30 years.	No
Jones '86 (Wales)	Interventions omitted	5 + 10 (BF guidance in hospital and after discharge).	BF at 4 weeks was significantly higher in the intervention group.	5.1 10.1
Jenner '88 (England)	1 prenatal home visit + 1 short visit after birth	As control + two extra prenatal home visits + 2-3 postnatal home visits (Step 10)	Antenatal and postnatal home visits associated with increased full BF at 3 months (p<.01)	10.1
Burkhalter '91 (Chile) [1, 4b, 6]	Pre-int: interventions omitted, hospital practices at birth not described	After: 3 + 10 (antenatal preparation and BF counselling after discharge).	Significant increase in full BF, especially at 5 and 6 months of age in intervention groups.	10.2
Nylander '91 (Norway) [4b, 6, 8]	Pre-int: interventions not commenced	After: 2 + 4 + 5 + partial 6 (formula and glucose water restricted) + 8.	Significant increase of full BF at 6 months after the BF promotion programme started.	6.1
Popkin '91 (Honduras)	Pre-int: routine use of prelacteal and formula feeds, mother-child separation	Mass media campaign and BF promotion programme in 3 major hospitals: steps 1 + 2 + 4-9.	Substantial increase in BF initiation and duration, especially in urban areas, despite changes in population characteristics that would have decreased BF rates	2.1
Long et al '95 (USA) [4]	Pre-int: routine prenatal care	3 + 10: antenatal and postnatal counselling by trained peer	Increase in BF at birth and at 3 months (non significant)	10.2

[a]: Numbers refer to Steps 1-10   BF: breastfeeding

Table 11.2. (Cont.) COMPARATIVE RESULTS OF EXPERIMENTAL STUDIES

COMBINED INTERVENTIONS - GROUPED

Study [Methodology limitations]	Control	Intervention[a]	General Results	Table
Alvarado '96 (Chile)	Health monitoring at health centre	3 + 10: home visits and group education by trained lay counsellors	Exclusive BF at 4 months significantly higher	10.2
Davies-Adetugbo '96 (Nigeria)	Routine prenatal care in PHC facilities and home visits (problems referred)	3 + 10: prenatal counselling + monthly postpartum home visits (most BF problems solved)	Improved knowledge and attitudes about BF, full BF at 4 months increased	10.2
Morrow '96 (Mexico)	Routine care in clinic (concurrent and historical controls)	I: 3 + 10, 3 home visits by trained lay counsellors (at end of pregnancy, soon after birth, and at the end of week 2) I: 3 + 10, 6 home visits by same trained lay counsellors (2 during pregnancy, 1 soon after birth, and at 2, 4 and 8 weeks)	Exclusive breastfeeding at 3 months significantly higher in intervention groups compared to controls, and significantly higher when comparing 6 home visits with 3 home visits	10.2
Lutter '97 (Brazil)	BF activities universally low	4-7, 10 (possibly 1, 2, 8, 9)	Exclusive BF was 53 days longer, according to survival analysis	No

[a]. Numbers refer to Steps 1-10   BF: breastfeeding

CONCLUSIONS AND RECOMMENDATIONS

The evidence for most of the Ten Steps to Successful Breastfeeding is substantial, even when each step is considered separately, and despite the inherent difficulties of randomization, when a mother's freedom of choice must be respected.

The most clearly established are the three steps concerning guidance and support for the mother. These are: Step 3, antenatal education; Step 5, showing mothers how to breastfeed; and Step 10, continuing support after discharge from hospital. They are the steps which can be the most difficult to implement adequately, and they are often the slowest to be introduced. They require skill, which needs training, and they take health worker time so they require revision of job descriptions. However, together they are among the most cost-effective of all health interventions, and efforts to include adequate support for breastfeeding mothers should be strengthened regardless of limitations of resources.

There is good evidence in principle for Step 4, which relates to early contact, though the optimal timing of a newborn's first breastfeed is probably not as restricted as the original wording of the step suggests. The most important part of the procedure is for the baby to have skin-to-skin contact with the mother from immediately after delivery until he or she spontaneously shows readiness to feed. This usually occurs within an hour of birth, though it may be at any time in the first two hours, or later if the mother received pethidine.

The evidence for Steps 7, rooming-in, and Step 8, demand feeding, which are easy to implement but difficult to separate from one another, is highly suggestive. There is no evidence supporting the contrary practices of scheduled feeding and nursery care. Demand feeding does not increase the risk of sore nipples; and rooming-in does not necessarily interfere with the mother's rest, and does not increase cross-infection.

Step 6, on the use of supplements, and Step 9, on the use of artificial teats and pacifiers, are also closely related. While many studies show a strong association between the use of supplements and artificial teats or pacifiers with premature cessation of breastfeeding, it is not easy to demonstrate a causal relationship, largely because of the difficulty of true randomization. However, if the use of supplements, teats and pacifiers are partly markers of mothers who have difficulties breastfeeding, or who lack confidence, then they are also an indication that health workers need more knowledge and skills to help mothers more effectively. Without adequate guidance and continuing support, the need to use supplements may not be overcome.

It remains probable that artificial feeds, teats and pacifiers do interfere physiologically with breastfeeding, and that its ready availability and use undermines a mother's confidence. Pacifiers and teats should rarely be needed in maternity facilities, and there is ample justification for not allowing infants to be given supplements except when there is an unavoidable medical reason, and for giving them when needed by cup rather than bottle. Some evidence suggests that when there is a clear medical indication, supplements may interfere with establishing breastfeeding less than when they are given without such an indication.

Two other points are clear in this connection. First, the provision of commercial discharge packs which contain samples of breastmilk substitutes adversely affects breastfeeding, and there is no justification for giving them. Second, discontinuing the provision of formula in maternity facilities has been shown to be one of the most cost-effective health interventions known.

There remain Steps 1 and 2, on policy and training, which are necessary for the implementation of all the others. Experience shows that without both strong policies and relevant training of staff, it is not possible to change practices.

With the advent of the Baby Friendly Hospital Initiative, a great deal of experience with different kinds of training has been gained. Although they can all have some effect, certain principles are apparent. Eighteen hours of training seems to be an absolute minimum, and a longer time is probably needed for effective increase in skills and change in attitude. Training needs to include a strong practical and clinical component, and not to be predominantly theoretical or classroom-based. Well organized clinical practice seems to change attitudes towards breastfeeding in a way that lectures do not.

In conclusion, the basic premise of the Baby Friendly Hospital Initiative, which requires all maternity facilities to implement the Ten Steps to Successful Breastfeeding, is valid. However, selective implementation of only some steps may be ineffective and discouraging. Exclusive breastfeeding will be most effectively increased and sustained when agreed policies and adequate practical training of staff are directed at implementing all the ten steps together, including continuing support for mothers in the community, and restriction of the availability of formula to situations in which there are clearly defined medical reasons.

Recommendations

1. Sufficient evidence exists for the effectiveness of the Ten Steps to Successful Breastfeeding, to fully justify extending the Baby Friendly Hospital Inititative, which is based on them, to all maternity facilities. Failure to make maternity services baby-friendly can no longer be considered defensible.

2. The 'Ten Steps' should be implemented together, and not expected to be effective when introduced incompletely or in isolation.

3. Health facilities should develop strong policies, covering all the 'Ten Steps' and including the restriction of free supplies of breastmilk substitutes, with appropriate arrangements for enforcement and supervision.

4. Training of health workers in relation to the 'Ten Steps' should be of adequate length and should include a strong practical component to ensure improvement in clinical and counselling skills. Training should also address the attitudes of health workers towards breastfeeding and the use of supplements.

5. Renewed efforts should be made to strengthen those steps which relate to education, guidance and support for mothers before and after delivery, including after discharge from hospital, as they are the most clearly effective interventions. Without education, guidance and support for mothers, implementation of the management steps such as rooming-in are likely to have only a limited effect. All mothers should have access to appropriate guidance and support throughout the breastfeeding period.

LIST OF REFERENCES

Alexander JM, Grant AM, Campbell MJ (1992) Randomised controlled trial of breast shells and Hoffman exercises for inverted and non-protractile nipples. *British medical journal*, 304:1030-1032.

Ali Z, Lowry M (1981) Early maternal-child contact: Effects on later behaviour. *Developmental medicine and child neurology*, 23:337-345.

Altobelli L, Baiocchi-Ureta N, Larson E (1991) A controlled trial to extend the duration of exclusive breastfeeding among low income mothers in Lima, Peru. Final report (unpublished). The Johns Hopkins University (Baltimore), Cayetano Heredia University (Lima) and The Population Council (New York).

Alvarado R et al (1996) Evaluation of a breastfeeding-support programme with health promoters' participation. *Food and nutrition bulletin*, 17(1):49-53.

Ardran GM, Kemp FH, Lind J (1958a) A cineradiographic study of bottle feeding. *British journal of radiology*, 31:11-22.

Ardran GM, Kemp FH, Lind J (1958b) A cineradiographic study of breast feeding. *British journal of radiology*, 31:156-162.

Armstrong HC (1990) Breastfeeding promotion: training of mid-level and outreach health workers. *International journal of gynecology and obstetrics* 31 (Suppl. 1):91-103.

Ashraf RN et al (1991) Breast feeding and protection against neonatal sepsis in a high risk population. *Archives of disease in childhood*, 66:488-490.

Avoa A, Fischer PR (1990) The influence of perinatal instruction about breast-feeding on neonatal weight loss. *Pediatrics*, 86(2):313-315.

Baranowski T et al (1983) Social support, social influence, ethnicity and the breastfeeding decision. *Social science and medicine*, 17(21):1599-1611.

Barros FC et al (1995a) Use of pacifiers is associated with decreased breast-feeding duration. *Pediatrics*, 95(4):497-499.

Barros FC et al (1995b) The impact of lactation centres on breastfeeding patterns, morbidity and growth: a birth cohort study. *Acta paediatrica*, 84:1221-1226.

Bathija CG, Anand RK (1987) Effect of perinatal motivation on breastfeeding in educated mothers. *Indian pediatrics*, 24:933-937.

Becker GE (1992) Breastfeeding knowledge of hospital staff in rural maternity units in Ireland. *Journal of human lactation*, 8(3):137-142.

Bergevin Y, Dougherty C, Kramer MS (1983) Do infant formula samples shorten the duration of breast-feeding? *Lancet*, I(8334):1148-1151.

Bliss MC et al (1997) The effect of discharge pack formula and breast pumps on breastfeeding duration and choice of infant feeding method. *Birth*, 24:90-97.

Blomquist HK et al (1994) Supplementary feeding in the maternity ward shortens the duration of breast feeding. *Acta paediatrica*, 83:1122-1126.

Bloom K et al (1982) II. Factors affecting the continuance of breast feeding. *Acta paediatrica Scandinavica*, Suppl 300:9-14.

Blum D, Feachem RG (1983) Measuring the impact of water supply and sanitation investments on diarrhoeal diseases: problems of methodology. *International journal of epidemiology*, 12(3):357-365.

Bradley JE, Meme J (1992) Breastfeeding promotion in Kenya: changes in health worker knowledge, attitudes and practices, 1982-89. *Journal of tropical pediatrics*, 38:228-234.

Breastfeeding counselling: A training course. Geneva, World Health Organization, 1993 (unpublished WHO documents WHO/CDR/93.3-6) and New York, UNICEF, 1993 (unpublished UNICEF documents UNICEF/NUT/93.1-4).

Bryant CA (1982) The impact of kin, friend and neighbor networks on infant feeding practices. *Social science and medicine*, 16:1757-1765.

Buranasin B (1991) The effects of rooming-in on the success of breastfeeding and the decline in abandonment of children. *Asia-Pacific journal of public health*, 5(3):217-220.

Burkhalter BR, Marin PS (1991) A demonstration of increased exclusive breastfeeding in Chile. *International journal of gynecology and obstetrics* 34:353-359.

Christensson K et al (1992) Temperature, metabolic adaptation and crying in healthy full-term newborns cared for skin-to-skin or in a cot. *Acta paediatrica*, 81:488-493.

Christensson K et al (1995) Separation distress call in the human neonate in the absence of maternal body contact. *Acta paediatrica*, 84:468-473.

Chua S et al (1994) Influence of breastfeeding and nipple stimulation on postpartum uterine activity. *British journal of obstetrics and gynaecology,*101:804-805.

Chung-Hey C (1993) Effects of home visits and telephone contacts on breastfeeding compliance in Taiwan. *Maternal-child nursing journal,* 21(3): 82-90.

Clements MS et al (1997) Influences on breastfeeding in southeast England. *Acta paediatrica,* 86:51-56.

Cracking the Code. Monitoring the International Code of Breast-milk Substitutes. Country profiles. London, The Interagency Group on Breastfeeding Monitoring, 1997.

Cronenwett L et al (1992) Single daily bottle use in the early weeks postpartum and breast-feeding outcomes. *Pediatrics,* 90(5):760-766.

Cunningham WE, Segree W (1990) Breast feeding promotion in an urban and a rural Jamaican hospital. *Social science and medicine,* 30(3):341-348.

Davies-Adetugbo AA (1996) Promotion of breast feeding in the community: impact of health education programme in rural communities in Nigeria. *Journal of diarrhoeal disease research,* 14(1):5-11.

Davies-Adetugbo AA (1997) Sociocultural factors and the promotion of exclusive breastfeeding in rural Yoruba communities of Osun State, Nigeria. *Social science and medicine,* 45 (1):113-125.

de Carvalho M, Hall M, Harvey D (1981) Effects of water supplementation on physiological jaundice in breast-fed babies. *Archives of disease in childhood,* 56(7):568-569.

de Carvalho M et al (1982a) Milk intake and frequency of feeding in breast fed infants. *Early human development,* 7:155-163

de Carvalho M, Klaus MH, Merkatz RB (1982b) Frequency of breast-feeding and serum bilirubin concentration. *American journal of diseases of children,* 136:737-738.

de Carvalho M et al (1983) Effect of frequent breast-feeding on early milk production and infant weight gain. *Pediatrics,* 72(3):307-311.

de Carvalho M, Robertson S, Klaus MH (1984) Does the duration and frequency of early breastfeeding affect nipple pain? *Birth,* 11:81-84.

de Carvalho M et al (1985) Frequency of milk expression and milk production by mothers of nonnursing premature neonates. *American journal of diseases of children,* 139:483-485.

de Château P, Wiberg B (1977a) Long-term effect on mother-infant behaviour of extra contact during the first hour post partum: II. A follow-up at three months. *Acta paediatrica Scandinavica,* 66:145-151.

de Château P et al (1977b) A study of factors promoting and inhibiting lactation. *Developmental medicine and child neurology,* 19:575-584.

de Zoysa I, Rea M, Martines J (1991) Why promote breastfeeding in diarrhoeal disease control programmes? *Health policy and planning,* 6(4):371-379.

Diaz S et al (1995) Breast-feeding duration and growth of fully breast-fed infants in a poor urban Chilean population. *American journal of clinical nutrition,* 62: 371-376.

Dix DN (1991) Why women decide not to breastfeed. *Birth,* 18:222-225.

Drane D (1996) The effect of use of dummies and teats on orofacial development. *Breastfeeding review,* 4(2):59-64.

Dungy C et al (1992) Effect of discharge samples on duration of breast-feeding. *Pediatrics,* 90(2):233-237.

Dungy C et al (1997) Hospital infant formula discharge packages. Do they affect the duration of breast-feeding?. *Archives of pediatric and adolescent medicine,* 151:724-729.

Elander G, Lindberg T (1984) Short mother-infant separation during first week of life influences the duration of breastfeeding. *Acta paediatrica Scandinavica,* 73:237-240.

Elander G, Lindberg T (1986) Hospital routines in infants with hyperbilirubinemia influence the duration of breastfeeding. *Acta paediatrica Scandinavica,* 75:708-712.

Entwisle DR, Doering SG, Reilly TW (1982) Sociopsychological determinants of women's breastfeeding behavior: A replication and extension. *American journal of orthopsychiatry,* 52(2):244-260.

Eregie CO (1997) Impact of the Baby Friendly Hospital Initiative: An observation from an African population. *International child health,* VIII(4):7-9.

Evans CJ, Lyons NB, Killien MG (1986) The effect of infant formula samples on breastfeeding practice. *Journal of obstetrics, gynecology and neonatal nursing* Sept/Oct:401-405.

Feinstein JM et al (1986) Factors related to early termination of breast-feeding in an urban population. *Pediatrics,* 78(2):210-215.

Fisher C The puerperium and breastfeeding. In: Marsh GN, ed. *Modern obstetrics in general practice.* Oxford, Oxford University Press, 1985: 325-348.

Fisher C, Inch S (1996) Nipple confusion - who is confused? *Journal of pediatrics,* 129(1):174.

Fishman C, Evans R, Jenks E (1988) Warm bodies, cool milk: Conflicts in post partum food choice for

Indochinese women in California. *Social science and medicine,* 26(11):1125-1132.

Forman MR. (1984) Review of research on the factors associated with choice and duration of infant feeding in less-developed countries. *Pediatrics,* 74(4), Supplement:667-694.

Frank DA et al (1987) Commercial discharge packs and breast-feeding counseling: Effects on infant feeding practices in a randomized trial. *Pediatrics,* 80(6):845-854.

Freed G Fraley JK, Schanler RJ (1992) Attitudes of expectant fathers regarding breast-feeding. *Pediatrics,* 90(2):224-227.

Freed G Fraley JK, Schanler RJ (1993) Accuracy of expectant mothers' predictions of fathers' attitudes regarding breast-feeding. *Journal of family practice,* 37(2):148-152.

Fukumoto M, Creed-Kanashiro H (1994) Congratulations to the mothers.*Dialogue on diarrhoea,* 59:4.

Garforth S, Garcia J (1989) Breast feeding policies in practice - "No wonder they get confused". *Midwifery,* 5:75-83.

Giugliani ERJ et al (1994) Effect of breastfeeding support from different sources on mother's decisions to breastfeed. *Journal of human lactation,* 10(3):157-161.

Glover J, Sandilands M (1990) Supplementation of breastfeeding infants and weight loss in hospital.*Journal of human lactation,* 6(4):163-166.

Gökçay G et al (1997) Ten steps for successful breast-feeding: assessment of hospital performance, its determinants and planning for improvement. *Child: care, health and development,* 23(2):187-200.

Gonzales RB (1990) A large scale rooming-in program in a developing country: the Dr. Jose Fabella Memorial Hospital experience. *International journal of gynecology and obstetrics,* 31(Supplement 1):31-34.

Graffy JP (1992) Mothers' attitudes to and experience of breast feeding: a primary care study.*British journal of general practice,* 42:61-64.

Gray-Donald K et al (1985) Effect of formula supplementation in the hospital on the duration of breastfeeding: a controlled clinical trial. *Pediatrics,* 75(3):514-518.

Grossman LK, Harter C, Kay A (1987) Postpartum lactation counseling for low-income women. *American journal of diseases of children,* 141(4):375.

Grossman LK et al (1990) The effect of postpartum lactation counseling on the duration of breast-feeding in low-income women. *American journal of diseases of children,* 144:471-474.

Guthrie GM et al (1985) Infant formula samples and breast feeding among Philippine urban poor. *Social science and medicine,* 20(7):713-717.

Haider R et al (1996) Breast-feeding counselling in a diarrhoeal disease hospital.*Bulletin of the World Health Organization,* 74(2):173-179.

Hall JM (1978) Influencing breastfeeding success. *Journal of obstetrics, gynecology and neonatal nursing* Nov-Dec:28-32.

Hally MR et al (1984) Factors influencing the feeding of first-born infants. *Acta paediatrica Scandinavica,* 73(1):33-39.

Hardy EE et al (1982) Breastfeeding promotion: Effect of an educational program in Brazil.*Studies in family planning,* 13(3):79-86.

Hartmann PE et al (1996) Breast development and control of milk synthesis. *Food and nutrition bulletin,* 17(4):292-302.

Heiberg Endresen E, Helsing E (1995) Changes in breastfeeding practices in Norwegian maternity wards: national surveys 1973, 1982 and 1991.*Acta paediatrica,* 84:719-724.

Hofmeyr GJ et al (1991) Companionship to modify the clinical birth environment: effects on progress and perceptions of labour, and breastfeeding.*British journal of obstetrics and gynaecology,* 98(8):756-764.

Hopkinson JM, Schanler RJ, Garza C (1988) Milk production by mothers of premature infants.*Pediatrics,* 81(6):815-820.

Horton S et al (1996) Breastfeeding promotion and priority setting in health. *Health policy and planning,* 11(2):156-168.

Høst A (1991) Importance of the first meal on the development of cow's milk allergy and intolerance.*Allergy proceedings,* 12(4):227-232.

Houston MJ et al (1981) Do breast feeding mothers get the home support they need? *Health bulletin,* 39(3):166-172.

Howie PW et al (1981) How long should a breast feed last?*Early human development,* 5:71-77.

Howie PW et al (1990) Protective effect of breast feeding against infection.*British medical journal,* 300:11-16.

Huffman SL (1984) Determinants of breastfeeding in developing countries: Overview and policy implications. *Studies in family planning,* 15(4):170-182.

Iker CE, Mogan J (1992) Supplementation of breastfed infants: Does continuing education for nurses make a difference? *Journal of human lactation*, 8(3):131-135.

Illingworth RS, Stone DGH (1952) Self-demand feeding in a maternity unit. *Lancet*, I(6710):683-687.

Inch S, Garforth S. Establishing and maintaining breastfeeding. In: Chalmers I, Enkin MW, Kierse M, eds. *Effective care in pregnancy and childbirth*. Oxford, Oxford University Press, 1989:1359-1374.

Inoue N, Sakashita R, Kamegai T (1995) Reduction of masseter muscle activity in bottle-fed babies. *Early human development*, 42:185-193.

Jackson EB, Wilkin LC, Auerbach H (1956) Statistical report on incidence and duration of breast feeding in relation to personal-social and hospital maternity factors. *Pediatrics*, 17(5):700-715.

Jamieson L (1994) Getting it together. *Nursing times*, 90(17):68-69.

Janke JR (1988) Breastfeeding duration following cesarean and vaginal births. *Journal of nurse-midwifery*, 33(4):159-164.

Janovsky K, Cassels A. Health policy and systems research: Issues, methods, priorities. In: Janovsky K., ed. *Health policy and systems development. An agenda for research.* Geneva, World Health Organization, 1996:11-23 (unpublished document WHO/SHS/NHP/96.1).

Jenner S (1988) The influence of additional information, advice and support on the success of breast feeding in working class primiparas. *Child: care, health and development,* 14:319-328.

Jones DA, West RR (1986) Effect of a lactation nurse on the success of breast-feeding: a randomised controlled trial. *Journal of epidemiology and community health,* 40:45-49.

Jones E (1994) Breastfeeding in the preterm infant. *Modern midwife,* 4(1):22-26.

Kaplowitz DD, Olson CM (1983) The effect of an education program on the decision to breastfeed. *Journal of nutrition education,* 15(2):61-65.

Kearney M, Cronenwett LR, Reinhardt R (1990) Cesarean delivery and breastfeeding outcomes. *Birth,* 17:97-103.

Keefe MR (1987) Comparison of neonatal nighttime sleep-wake patterns in nursery versus rooming-in environments. *Nursing research,* 36(3):140-144.

Keefe MR (1988) The impact of infant rooming-in on maternal sleep at night. *Journal of obstetrics, gynecology and neonatal nursing,* March-April:122-126.

Kistin N et al (1990) Breast-feeding rates among black urban low-income women: effect of prenatal education. *Pediatrics,* 86(5):741-746.

Kistin N et al (1994) Effect of peer counselors on breastfeeding initiation, exclusivity, and duration among low-income urban women. *Journal of human lactation,* 10(1):11-15.

Klaus MH (1987) The frequency of suckling. *Obstetrics and gynecology clinics of North America,* 14(3):623-633.

Koktürk T, Zetterström R (1989) The promotion of breastfeeding and maternal attitudes. *Acta paediatrica Scandinavica,* 78:817-823.

Kurinij N et al (1984) Predicting duration of breastfeeding in a group of urban primiparae. *Ecology of food and nutrition,* 15:281-291.

Kurinij N, Shiono PH (1991) Early formula supplementation of breast-feeding. *Pediatrics,* 88(4):745-750.

Labbok MH, Hendershot GE (1987) Does breastfeeding protect against malocclusion? An analysis of the 1981 Child Health Supplement to the National Health Interview Survey. *American journal of preventive medicine,* 3(4):227-232.

Labbok MH, Simon SR (1988) A community study of a decade of in-hospital breast-feeding: implications for breast-feeding promotion. *American journal of preventive medicine,* 4(2):62-66.

Lang S, Lawrence CJ, Orme RL'E (1994) Cup feeding: an alternative method of infant feeding. *Archives of disease in childhood,* 71:365-369.

Lawrence RA (1982) Practices and attitudes toward breast-feeding among medical professionals. *Pediatrics,* 70(6):912-920.

Lazzaro E, Anderson J, Auld G (1995) Medical professionals' attitudes towards breastfeeding. *Journal of human lactation,* 11(2):97-101.

Leefsma M, Habatsky T. The influence of hospital routine on successful breastfeeding. In: Freier S, Eidelman AL, eds. *International Symposium on Breastfeeding. Human milk – It's biological and social value.* Amsterdam, Excerpta Medica, 1980:309-313.

Leite A, Puccini R, Atallah A, Cunha A, Machado M, Capiberibe A, Rodrigues R. Impact on breastfeeding practices promoted by lay counselors: a randomized and controlled clinical trial. In: Feinstein AR, Vandenbrouke JP, eds. *Abstracts of the Inclen 15th global meeting of the International Clinical Epidemiology Network.* Querétaro, Mexico, Journal of Clinical Epidemiology, 1998, 51(supplement 1):10S.

Levitt C et al (1996) Breast-feeding policies and practices in Canadian hospitals providing maternity care.

Canadian Medical Association Journal, 155(2):181-188.

Lizarraga JL et al (1992) Psychosocial and economic factors associated with infant feeding intentions of adolescent mothers. *Journal of adolescent health,* 13:676-681.

Long DG et al (1995) Peer counselor program increases breastfeeding rates in Utah native American WIC population. *Journal of human lactation,* 11(4):279-284.

Long L (1995) Breastfeeding workshops: a focus on knowledge, skills and attitudes. *British journal of midwifery,* 3(10):540-544.

Lundgren R et al (1992) The promotion of breastfeeding and birth spacing in rural areas. Final technical report (unpublished document). Asociacion Hondureña de Lactancia Materna (AHLACMA) and the Population Council.

Lutter CK et al (1997) The effectiveness of a hospital-based program to promote exclusive breast-feeding among low-income women in Brazil. *American journal of public health,* 87(4):659-663.

McBryde A, Durham NC (1951) Compulsory rooming-in on the ward and private newborn service at Duke hospital. *Journal of the American Medical Association,* 145(9):625-628.

McDivitt JA et al (1993) The impact of the healthcom mass media campaign on timely initiation of breastfeeding in Jordan. *Studies in family planning,* 24(5):295-309.

McKenna JJ, Mosko SS, Richard CA (1997) Bedsharing promotes breastfeeding. *Pediatrics,* 100(2):214-219.

McLorg PA, Bryant CA (1989) Influence of social network members and health care professionals on infant feeding practices of economically disadvantaged mothers. *Medical anthropology,* 10:265-278.

MAIN Trial Collaborative Group (1994) Preparing for breastfeeding: treatment of inverted and non-protractile nipples in pregnancy. *Midwifery,* 10:200-214.

Manning DJ, Coughlin RP, Poskitt EME (1985) Candida in mouth or dummy? *Archives of disease in childhood,* 60:381-382.

Mapata S, Djauhariah AM, Dasril D (1988) A study comparing rooming-in with separate nursing. *Paediatrica Indonesiana,* 28:116-123.

Margen S et al. *Infant feeding in Mexico. A study of health facility and mothers' practices in three regions.* Nestlé Infant Formula Audit Commission. California, PRINTEAM, 1991.

Martin-Calama J et al (1997) The effect of feeding glucose water to breastfeeding newborns on weight, body temperature, blood glucose, and breastfeeding duration. *Journal of human lactation,* 13(3):209-213.

Martines JC, Ashworth A, Kirkwood B (1989) Breast-feeding among the urban poor in southern Brazil: reasons for termination in the first 6 months of life. *Bulletin of the World Health Organization,* 67(2):151-161.

Mathew OP, Bhatia J (1989) Sucking and breathing patterns during breast- and bottle-feeding in term neonates. *American journal of diseases of children,* 143:588-592.

Matich JR, Sims LS (1992) A comparison of social support variables between women who intend to breast or bottle feed. *Social science and medicine,* 34(8):919-927.

Maza ,IC et al (1997) *Sustainability of a Community-Based Mother-to-Mother Support Project in the Peri-Urban Areas of Guatemala City. A La Leche League Study.* Published for La Leche League International and the U.S. Agency for International Development by the Basic Support for Institutionalizing Child Survival (BASICS) Project. Arlington, Va.

Meara H (1976) La Leche League in the United States: A key to successful breast-feeding in a non-supportive culture. *Journal of nurse-midwifery,* 21(1):20-26.

Meier P (1988) Bottle- and breast-feeding: effects on transcutaneous oxygen pressure and temperature in preterm infants. *Nursing research,* 37(1):36-41

Meier P (1994) Breast feeding the premature baby: a research review. *News brief,* 9(1):2-5.

Milnes AR (1996) Description and epidemiology of nursing caries. *Journal of public health dentistry,* 56(1):38-50.

Mohrbacher N, Stock J. *The breastfeeding answer book,* Franklin, Illinois, La Leche League International, 1991.

Mongeon M et al (1995) Essai controlé d'un soutien téléphonique régulier donné par une bénévole sur le déroulement et l'issue de l'allaitement. *Canadian journal of public health,* 86(2):124-127.

Morrow AL et al The effectiveness of home-based counseling to promote exclusive breastfeeding among Mexican mothers. In: *Exclusive breastfeeding promotion: a summary of findings from EPB's applied research program (1992-1996).* Wellstart International's Expanded Promotion of Breastfeeding (EPB) Program (unpublished document).

Morse JM, Jehle C, Gamble D (1992) Initiating breastfeeding: a world survey of the timing of postpartum breastfeeding. *Breastfeeding review,* May:210-216.

Musoke RN (1990) Breastfeeding promotion: feeding the low birth weight infant. *International journal of gynecology and obstetrics,* 31 (Suppl. 1):57-59.

Neifert M et al (1988) Factors influencing breast-feeding among adolescents. *Journal of adolescent health care,* 9:470-473.

Neifert M, Lawrence R, Seacat J (1995) Nipple confusion: toward a formal definition. *Journal of pediatrics,* 126:S125-129.

Neyzi O et al (1991a) An educational intervention on promotion of breast-feeding. *Pediatric and perinatal epidemiology,* 5:286-298.

Neyzi O et al (1991b) An educational intervention on promotion of breast-feeding complemented by continuing support. *Pediatric and perinatal epidemiology,* 5:299-303.

Nicoll A, Ginsburg R, Tripp JH (1982) Supplementary feeding and jaundice in newborns. *Acta paediatrica Scandinavica,* 71:759-761.

Niemelä M, Uhari M, Möttönen M (1995) A pacifier increases the risk of recurrent acute otitis media in children in day care centers. *Pediatrics,* 96(5):884-888.

Nissen E et al (1995) Effects of maternal pethidine on infants' developing breast feeding behaviour. *Acta paediatrica,* 84:140-145.

Nissen E et al (1996) Different patterns of oxytocin, prolactin but not cortisol release during breastfeeding in women delivered by Caesarean section or by the vaginal route. *Early human development,* 45:103-118.

Nissen E et al (1997) Effects of routinely given pethidine during labour on infants' developing breastfeeding behaviour. Effects of dose-delivery time interval and various concentrations of pethidine/norpethidine in cord plasma. *Acta paediatrica,* 86:201-208.

Norr KF, Roberts JE, Freese U (1989) Early post-partum rooming-in and maternal attachment behaviors in a group of medically indigent primiparas. *Journal of nurse-midwifery,* 34(2):85-91.

Nowak AJ, Smith WL, Erenberg A (1994) Imaging evaluation of artificial nipples during bottle feeding. *Archives of pediatrics and adolescent medicine,* 148:40-42.

Nylander G et al (1991) Unsupplemented breastfeeding in the maternity ward. Positive longterm effects. *Acta obstetrica gynecologica Scandinavica,* 70:205-209.

Nyqvist KH, Ewald U (1997) Successful breast feeding in spite of early mother-baby separation for neonatal care. *Midwifery,* 13:24-31.

O'Connor S et al (1980) Reduced incidence of parenting inadequacy following roomingin. *Pediatrics,* 66(2):176-182.

Perez-Escamilla R et al (1992) Effect of the maternity ward system on the lactation success of low-income urban Mexican women. *Early human development,* 31:25-40.

Perez-Escamilla R et al (1993) Determinants of lactation performance across time in an urban population from Mexico. *Social science and medicine,* 37(8):1069-1078.

Perez-Escamilla R et al (1994) Infant feeding policies in maternity wards and their effect on breast-feeding success: an analytical overview. *American journal of public health,* 84(1):89-97.

Perez-Escamilla R, Maulén-Radovan I, Dewey KG (1996) The association between cesarean delivery and breast-feeding outcomes among Mexican women. *American journal of public health,* 86(6):832-836.

Perez-Escamilla R et al (1996) Prelacteal feeds are negatively associated with breast-feeding outcomes in Honduras. *Journal of nutrition,* 126:2765-2773.

Pichaipat V et al (1992) An intervention model for breast feeding in Maharat Nakhon Ratchasima hospital. *Southeast Asean journal of tropical medicine and public health,* 23(3):439-443.

Popkin BM et al (1983) Breast-feeding determinants in low-income countries. *Medical anthropology,* 7(1):1-31.

Popkin BM, Yamamoto ME, Griffin CC (1985) Breast-feeding in the Philippines: the role of the health sector. *Journal of biosocial science,* Supplement 9:99-125.

Popkin BM et al (1991) An evaluation of a national breast-feeding promotion programme in Honduras. *Journal of biosocial science,* 23:5-21.

Powers NG, Naylor AJ, Wester RA (1994) Hospital policies: Crucial to breastfeeding success. *Seminars in perinatology,* 18(6):517-524.

Procianoy RS et al (1983) The influence of roomingin on breastfeeding. *Journal of tropical pediatrics,* 29:112-114.

Promoting breast-feeding in health facilities. A short course for administrators and policy-makers. Geneva, World Health Organization and Wellstart International, 1996 (unpublished document WHO/NUT/96.3).

Protecting, promoting and supporting breast-feeding: The special role of maternity services. A joint WHO/UNICEF statement. Geneva, World Health Organization, 1989.

Pugin E et al (1996) Does prenatal breastfeeding skills group education increase the effectiveness of a comprehensive breastfeeding promotion program? *Journal of human lactation,* 12(1):15-19.

Rajan L (1993) The contribution of professional support, information and consistent correct advice to successful breast feeding. *Midwifery*, 9:197-209.

Rajan L (1994) The impact of obstetric procedures and analgesia/anaesthesia during labour and delivery on breast feeding. *Midwifery*, 10:87-103.

Rea MF, Venancio SI (1998) Manejo clinico e aconselhamento em amamentaçao: avaliaçao de um treinamento. *Jornal de pediatria*.(submitted).

Reiff MI, Essock-Vitale SM (1985) Hospital influences on early infant-feeding practices. *Pediatrics*, 76:872-879.

Relucio-Clavano N (1981) The results of a change in hospital practices. A paediatrician's campaign for breastfeeding in the Philippines. *Assignment children*, 55/56:139-165.

Righard L, Alade MO (1990) Effect of delivery room routines on success of first breastfeed. *Lancet*, 336(8723):1105-1107.

Righard L, Alade MO (1992) Sucking technique and its effect on success of breastfeeding.*Birth*, 19:185-189.

Righard L, Alade MO (1997) Breastfeeding and the use of pacifiers.*Birth*, 24:116-120.

Riordan J. *A practical guide to breastfeeding*, Boston, Jones & Bartlett, 1991.

Rosenblatt JS (1994) Psychobiology of maternal behaviour: contribution to clinical understanding of maternal behaviour among humans.*Acta paediatrica supplement*, 397:3-8.

Rush J, Chalmers I, Enkin M. Care of the new mother and baby. In: Chalmers I, Enkin MW, Kierse M, eds. *Effective care in pregnancy and childbirth*. Oxford, 1989:1333-1346.

Saadeh R, Akré J (1996) Ten steps to successful breastfeeding: A summary of the rationale and scientific evidence. *Birth*, 23:154-160.

Salariya EM, Easton PM, Cater JI (1978) Duration of breast-feeding after early initiation and frequent feeding. *Lancet*, II(8100):1141-1143.

Saner G et al (1985) Promotion of breastfeeding in the postpartum mother. *Turkish journal of pediatrics*, 27(2):63-68.

Sanghvi TG. Improving the cost-effectiveness of breastfeeding promotion in maternity services. Summary of the USAID/LAC HNS study in Latin America (1992-1995). (Unpublished document; available on request from WELLSTART, 3333 K Street NW, Washington, DC 20007 USA. Telephone (202) 298-7979.)

Saunders S, Carroll J (1988) Post-partum breastfeeding support: Impact on duration.*Journal of the American Dietetic Association*, 88(2):213-215.

Schubiger G, Schwarz U, Tönz O (1997) UNICEF/WHO baby-friendly hospital initiative: does the use of bottles and pacifiers in the neonatal nursery prevent successful breastfeeding?*European journal of pediatrics*, 156:874-877.

Simopoulos AP, Grave GD (1984) Factors associated with the choice and duration of infant-feeding practice. *Pediatrics*, 74(4) Supplement:603-614.

Sio JO et al (1987) Oral candida: is dummy carriage the culprit?*Archives of disease in childhood*, 62:406-420.

Slaven S, Harvey D (1981) Unlimited suckling time improves breast feeding.*Lancet*, I(8216):392-393.

Sloper K, McKean L, Baum JD (1975) Factors influencing breast feeding.*Archives of disease in childhood*, 50:165-170.

Snell BJ et al (1992) The association of formula samples given at hospital discharge with the early duration of breastfeeding. *Journal of human lactation*, 8(2):67-72.

Sosa R et al. The effect of early mother-infant contact on breast feeding, infection and growth. In: *Ciba Foundation Symposium No. 45 (new series): Breastfeeding and the mother* Amsterdam, the Netherlands, Elsevier Publishing Co., 1976:179-193.

Stokamer CL (1990) Breastfeeding promotion efforts: why some do not work. *International journal of gynecology and obstetrics*, 31(Suppl 1):61-65.

Strachan-Lindenberg C, Cabrera-Artola R, Jimenez V (1990) The effect of early post-partum mother-infant contact and breastfeeding promotion on the incidence and continuation of breast-feeding.*International journal of nursing studies*, 27(3):179-186.

Suradi R (1988) Rooming-in for babies born by caesarean section in Dr. Cipto Mangunkusumo General Hospital Jakarta. *Paediatrica Indonesiana*, 28:124-132.

Taylor A (1998) Monitoring the International Code of Marketing of Breastmilk Substitutes: an epidemiological study in four countries. *British medical journal*, 316: 1117-1122.

Taylor PM et al (1985) II. Extra early mother-infant contact and duration of breast-feeding.*Acta paediatrica Scandinavica*, Suppl 316:15-22.

Taylor PM, Maloni JA, Brown DR (1986) Early suckling and prolonged breastfeeding.*American journal of diseases of children*, 140:151-154.

The Global Criteria for the WHO/UNICEF Baby Friendly Hospital Initiative. In: Baby Friendly Hospital

Initiative. Part II. Hospital level implementation. WHO/UNICEF, 1992.

Thomson ME, Hartsock TG, Larson C (1979) The importance of immediate postnatal contact: its effect on breastfeeding. *Canadian family physician*, 25:1374-1378.

Tully SB, Bar-Haim Y, Bradley RL (1995) Abnormal tympanography after supine bottle feeding. *Journal of pediatrics*, 126:S105-S111.

Valdes V et al (1993) The impact of a hospital and clinic-based breastfeeding promotion programme in a middle class urban environment. *Journal of tropical pediatrics*, 39:142-151.

Valdes V et al (1995) The effects on professional practices of a three-day course on breastfeeding. *Journal of human lactation*, 11(3):185-190.

Verronen P et al (1980) Promotion of breast feeding: effect on neonates of change of feeding routine at a maternity unit. *Acta paediatrica Scandinavica*, 69:279-282.

Victora CG et al (1987) Evidence for the protection by breast-feeding against infant deaths from infectious diseases in Brazil. *Lancet*, II(8554):319-322.

Victora CG et al (1990) Caesarean section and duration of breast feeding among Brazilians. *Archives of disease in childhood*, 65:632-634.

Victora CG et al (1993) Use of pacifiers and breastfeeding duration. *Lancet*, 341(8842):404-406.

Victora CG et al (1997) Pacifier-use and short breastfeeding duration: cause, consequence or coincidence? *Pediatrics*, 99(3):445-453.

Waldenstrom U, Swenson A (1991) Rooming-in at night in the portpartum ward. *Midwifery*, 7:82-89.

Waldenström U, Nilsson C-A (1994) No effect of birth centre care on either duration or experience of breast feeding, but more complications: findings from a randomised controlled trial. *Midwifery*, 10:8-17.

Westin JB (1990) Ingestion of carcinogenic N-nitrosamines by infants and children. *Archives of environmental health*, 45(6):359-363.

Westphal MF et al (1995) Breast-feeding training for health professionals and resultant institutional changes. *Bulletin of the World Health Organization*, 73(4):461-468.

Widstrom A-M et al (1987) Gastric suction in healthy newborn infants. *Acta paediatrica Scandinavica*, 76:566-572.

Widstrom A-M et al (1990) Short-term effects of early suckling and touch of the nipple on maternal behaviour. *Early human development*, 21:153-163.

Widstrom A-M, Thingström-Paulsson J (1993) The position of the tongue during rooting reflexes elicited in newborn infants before the first suckle. *Acta paediatrica*, 82:281-283.

Wilde CJ Prentice A, Peaker M (1995) Breast-feeding: matching supply with demand in human lactation. *Proceedings of the Nutrition Society*, 54: 401-406.

Wiles L (1984) The effect of prenatal breastfeeding education on breastfeeding success and maternal perception of the infant. *Journal of obstetrics, gynecology and neonatal nursing* July/Aug:253-257.

Williams AF (1997) Hypoglycaemia of the newborn: a review. *Bulletin of the World Health Organization*, 75(3):261-290.

Williamson IG, Dunleavey J, Robinson D (1994) Risk factors in otitis media with effusion. A 1 year case control study in 5-7 year old children. *Family practice*, 11(3):271-274.

Wilmoth TA, Elder JP (1995) An assessment of research on breastfeeding promotion strategies in developing countries. *Social science and medicine*, 41(4):579-594.

Winikoff B et al (1986) Dynamics of infant feeding: Mothers, professionals, and the institutional context in a large urban hospital. *Pediatrics*, 77(3):357-365.

Winikoff B et al (1987) Overcoming obstacles to breast-feeding in a large municipal hospital: Applications of lessons learned. *Pediatrics*, 80(3):423-433.

Woolridge M (1986a) The 'anatomy' of infant sucking. *Midwifery*, 2(4):164-171.

Woolridge MW (1986b) Aetiology of sore nipples. *Midwifery*, 2(4):172-176.

Woolridge MW, Baum JD (1993) Recent advances in breast feeding. *Acta paediatrica Japonica*, 35:1-12.

Woolridge MW (1996) Problems of establishing lactation. *Food and nutrition bulletin*, 17(4):316-323.

Wright A, Rice S, Wells S (1996) Changing hospital practices to increase the duration of breastfeeding. *Pediatrics*, 97(5):669-675.

Yamauchi Y, Yamanouchi I (1990a) Breast-feeding frequency during the first 24 hours after birth in full-term neonates. *Pediatrics*, 86(2):171-175.

Yamauchi Y, Yamanouchi I (1990b) The relationship between roomingin/not rooming-in and breast-feeding variables. *Acta paediatrica Scandinavica*, 79:1017-1022.

LIST OF ABBREVIATIONS

BF: Breastfeeding
EBF: Exclusive breastfeeding
HWs: Health workers
OR: Odds ratio
RR: Relative risk
RI: Rooming-in

LIST OF METHODOLOGICAL LIMITATIONS

1.   Inadequate control: no baseline data or between-group differences
2.   Confounding variables not controlled
3.   Self-selection of participants
4.   High (more than 10%) attrition rate unevenly distributed
5.   Undetermined internal validity: unreported attrition, poorly documented methodology or unpublished brief communication.
6.   One-to-one comparison
7.   Long recall period
8.   Unclear definition of breastfeeding indicators
9.   Based on planned breastfeeding behaviour as opposed to actual practice